Roadmap for College Admissions

Step-By-Step Directions for Success

Bina, Vinay, and
Sheila Chandrasekhara

A SCARECROWEDUCATION BOOK

The Scarecrow Press, Inc.
Lanham, Maryland, and Oxford
2003

A ScarecrowEducation Book

Published in the United States of America by Scarecrow Press, Inc.
A Member of the Rowman & Littlefield Publishing Group
4720 Boston Way, Lanham, Maryland 20706
www.scarecroweducation.com

PO Box 317, Oxford, OX2 9RU, UK

British Library Cataloguing in Publication Information Available

Library of Congress Cataloging-in-Publication Data

Chandrasekhara, Bina, 1953–
    Roadmap for college admissions : step-by-step directions for
success / Bina, Vinay, and Sheila Chandrasekhara.
        p.   cm.
    "A Scarecrow Education book."
    ISBN 0-8108-4497-4 (pbk. : alk. paper)
    1. Universities and colleges—United States—Admission.   2. College
choice—United States.   I. Chandrasekhara, Vinay.   II. Chandrasekhara,
Sheila, 1982–
    III. Title.
    LB2351.2 .C465   2003
    378.1'61'0973—dc21
                                                            2002010297

∞ ™The paper used in this publication meets the minimum requirements
of American National Standard for Information Sciences—Permanence of
Paper for Printed Library Materials, ANSI/NISO Z39.48-1992.
Manufactured in the United States of America.

CONTENTS

PREFACE

Students dream about going to a college of their first choice, a college that furthers their academic and personal goals. Although their choices may be different, the grueling, thrilling, devastating, and gratifying feelings surrounding the experience that all parents and students go through are the same. As parents, we want what is best for our children. Every year it makes us sad to see so many students from our high school disappointed with college admissions. Unfortunately, many of these competent students have minimal knowledge about the admissions process, unnecessarily diminishing their chances in an already extremely selective process. If students had the opportunity to understand and make the best use of their resources, they could maximize their chances of admission. We say this from firsthand experience, as our family knows this process well.

Not too long ago we discovered the difficult and surprising path to the college of our son's choice. Surely my son, Vinay, was one of those candidates who had it all: a good SAT score, class president, valedictorian, and MVP of the varsity tennis team. He was greatly respected by his teachers and received stellar recommendation letters. He even excelled in several college courses that he took when he was still in high school, including pre-med courses such as the history of medicine and biochemistry at Johns Hopkins. We confidently assumed that he would be accepted wherever he applied. We certainly had to reevaluate that assumption. Much to our surprise, although he was accepted by a few well-known schools such as Johns Hopkins and Swarthmore, where he was selected as a semifinalist McCabe scholar, several highly selective colleges rejected him, and others placed him on their waiting list. Yet we had been so confident that he could get into any college of his choice! We did not understand. We felt that our son had done everything possible to prepare and motivate himself for college. Though we were happy that he had been accepted by some of these top colleges, he was disappointed that he had not been accepted by more of the highly selective colleges that he wanted to attend. Like all parents, we wanted what was best for our child, but by this time we had run out of resources and did not know what to do next.

What did we learn from this? In retrospect, we realized that there was a lot more that we could have done to prepare for the admissions game.

We could have paid attention to little details, such as making sure that the recommendations were sent promptly. We could have focused more on the essays assigned on the applications, choosing a topic that actually reflected our son's true personality. We also realized that describing participation in a few activities with significant dedication or leadership roles matters a lot more than simply citing a laundry list of activities with minimal commitment. As Rochelle Sharpe states in a recent edition of the *Wall Street Journal*, "The college-admissions game rules have changed. After decades of looking for well rounded 'Renaissance kids' competitive colleges are clamoring for something different: passion for a single pursuit" (W1). Today's admissions officers look for signs of initiative and motivation through strong commitment to a few well-chosen activities. "We realized one of the better predicators of success is the ability to dedicate oneself to a task and do it well," says Lee Stetson, dean of admissions at the University of Pennsylvania (Sharpe, W1). We could have better succeeded by understanding all of the factors affecting the consideration of an applicant by an admissions officer. Then we could have closely examined each of these aspects and checked to see if anything could have been done differently.

After our son graduated from high school, we began the process all over again with my daughter, Sheila, who, like my son, also had good credentials. But this time our approach was proactive. Our children attended a large public school on the Eastern Shore of Maryland that did not provide much assistance in college counseling; therefore we realized that we must take an active role in educating ourselves about this process. We thoroughly read all the publications on college admissions we could find to get the most updated information on admissions criteria. We took many campus tours, scheduled on-campus interviews, attended several information sessions, talked to numerous admissions officers, and spoke to other students and parents who had just gone through a similar process. Basically, as with any major purchase, we took steps to become an informed consumer. Our daughter applied for early action to three schools: Georgetown, MIT, and Harvard. (It was the first year that applying to more than one school for early action was allowed, resulting in more applicants per school.) These new opportunities meant fierce competition with a strong applicant pool, making the admissions criteria for early action even harder. Much to our delight, our daughter was accepted by every college to which she applied.

What was the difference between my two children's application processes? Both went to the same public school, both had similar grades, and both were valedictorians. Both played sports and assumed leadership positions. The difference was the way we prepared and assisted our children during this crucial time. The first time around, with our son, we as parents had not educated ourselves about the application process. We did not understand what admissions officers were looking for in an applicant. Most importantly, we underestimated the strength of the applicant pool.

Once we were aware of the strength of the competition, we realized that we must present the applicant's profile in a manner that made him or her stand out from the rest of the pool. It is not just the quality or the quantity of credentials, but the way the student is marketed to the admissions committee that achieves individual success. As with any desired product, it is the package that first attracts attention. It is not the steak but the sizzle that makes it enticing. To be successful, a student must have both credentials and knowledge about the admissions process.

Although we have been blessed in successfully accomplishing our goals of sending our children to top colleges, the experiences of getting there were completely different. With my son, we went through the process without much knowledge concerning college admissions. Our struggles resembled a bumpy ride through new and unfamiliar terrain, trying to reach an objective without any instructions. Although our persistence and perseverance paid off and he was admitted to MIT, going through the process the second time with our daughter was far more rewarding in every way that we could imagine. Since we were well informed, the journey was like reaching a destination with a road map and directions and knowing exactly what turns to take. (She was admitted by early action to Harvard.) Finally, it also slowly occurred to us that instead of students struggling to hold to a nearly impossible standard, they could concentrate on fully understanding the process and strategically plan accordingly. Only then would they be able to use this admissions process as their opportunity to market and paint the best possible portrait of themselves.

Taking this path as informed applicants and parents, we realized that there is an ocean of in-depth information on college admissions, that it can be puzzling, and that there was not one source that clearly and succinctly summarized this process. Sometimes, an overwhelming volume of material can be fragmented, with sources at times contradicting each other as they are discovered. This is a personal account of a family who has gone through the experience, absorbed the conflicting possibilities, and distilled the necessary imperatives. As we came to understand, in retrospect, the rules of the admissions game, we came to realize what motivates us to write a user-friendly guide and share all the essential and functional information that we have gained by successfully following this course of action. We are aware that very often high school students and parents have demanding lifestyles, and we know firsthand that the application process is not easy. Very often families do not have time to read a fat book on college admissions. Instead they may only have time to read what is necessary. While it is vital that parents and prospective college students read this book at their own pace, it is also important that they read the entire book thoroughly at least once. Points to remember at the end of most chapters have been prepared to assist readers with a summary of what each section covers, providing a quick reference for busy readers.

The main purpose of this book is to give students and parents a comprehensive outline of what they can expect at the different stages of the admissions planning process, such as what to expect from college visits or how to plan important test dates throughout a student's academic career. This text can guide hopeful college students throughout their high school years with easily understood practical tips and information, thus making it possible for students to create their own strategic plans to navigate the admissions process smoothly. This book does not guarantee success, but by gaining a better understanding into the admissions process readers may greatly enhance their chances of attending the college of their choice.

ACKNOWLEDGMENTS

Thank you to Dr. John Wenke, whose professional perspective helped us to handle the hurdles of publishing a text; to Liz Mulford, who patiently walked us through the process; and to Dr. Memo Diriker, who familiarized us with the process of writing.

I (Bina) would like to thank my husband, Kota Chandrasekhara, M.D., who has been very supportive throughout our twenty-five years of marriage. I also thank my children, Vinay and Sheila, for providing me with this wonderful experience that led us all to write this book. The greatest gift I can give to my children—and all children—is the gift of empowerment through education.

This book is a tribute to parents and guardians, who bear a great responsibility in raising children today. This book is written for all the students who take their preliminary steps toward college education. The process of writing this book was a gratifying experience. Our motivation partly comes from our strong desire to help youth, and what better way to help them than by providing self-empowering suggestions for how to achieve their educational goals? My motivation also comes from my need to encourage all parents, especially mothers, to realize that the so-called empty nest is not the end of the world. Do not underestimate your potential. There is a whole world out there that needs your help. We just have to open our hearts and embrace it.

INTRODUCTION

Balancing the college application process with schoolwork, extracurricular activities, and other responsibilities is a daunting task. This schedule can be an overwhelming experience for students and their parents, but it is all worth the effort once students are admitted to a college of their choice. Early in the process students must have a sense of direction and stay focused. The earlier students begin preparing for college, the better their chances for success will be. Start planning your application strategy early.

Every year a record number of college hopefuls apply to colleges and compete in the same admissions pool, making this process seem nearly impossible for young students. Thus, students should not embark on this journey alone; they should seek the advice and assistance of parents, guardians, and counselors. It is very important for parents and students to have an in-depth knowledge of the admissions procedure; they should take advantage of all of the available information and services. By becoming educated consumers, parents and students will be able to make appropriate decisions for themselves. The critical factor, then, is to apply the information learned to your individual requirements and thereby plan wisely and carefully: planning is the key to a successful college admissions process.

Readers should ask themselves questions about what college is right for their needs and personalities. When choosing a college, what one should seek is a good match. Does a specific school have all the educational opportunities for you to explore? It is a good idea to narrow the list of colleges to the ones that suit your personality and academic plans. What are your chances of admission?

No matter the personal choice of school, many people believe that whatever college a student attends, he or she will eventually adjust to the university and enjoy the undergraduate experience. However, where you go to college is very critical to your development as a person and has an enormous impact on your future. Your college is where you will be spending the next four years of your life. It will have an influence on whom you meet and with whom you interact. Eventually, it may influence your prospective major and career goals. You should remember that you are making plans not only for college but also for your future. Starting your college search early in high school will increase your chances of finding a school that is right for you.

Parents and guardians are the most influential people and the driving force behind the vital decisions determined throughout their child's admission process. Parents should take the initiative to guide their child and also know when to step back when the child shows signs of independence and capability. Remember when your child turned sixteen and got a driver's license? In order to encourage your child and boost self-esteem and confidence, you let the new driver take over the steering wheel. You had no choice but to trust your child. But although you were not driving, you were only a passenger in your child's car, you still gave directions and guidance as needed. Now, too, as a parent your part is to let your child know that you have confidence in his or her capabilities for completing these applications. Encourage your child to believe in him- or herself. Our children knew that they could count on us for all the moral support that they needed and could come to us anytime for our suggestions. They also knew when we would let them take their own initiative since we trusted them to make responsible choices.

As parents, your part in the admission process is crucial, yet at times it can be an especially puzzling and overwhelming experience. The experience of admissions can be exciting, intimidating, confusing, and demanding, for both students and parents. We often wished that there were an easy-to-follow book for students with a step-by-step admissions guide, to help them throughout their high school years, where points are clearly outlined instead of being presented in diffuse form. As we learned more information and gained more experience, we wrote a concise list of main points that we could use as a quick reference. After a while, we realized that we had compiled so many helpful points from our experience that we wanted to share them with all high school students who are serious about going to college.

This book is a culmination of all of our research and experiences relating to successfully going through the admissions process and having our children admitted to the top universities of their choice. This book contains all the practical tips and strategies that we found to be helpful while my children were preparing for college admissions. This book is partly written by myself and partly written by my children, and it is addressed to both parents or guardians and students. We would encourage readers to examine this book thoroughly before the admissions process, as it includes admissions plans that can be followed as early as the ninth grade. For quick reference, readers can refer to the main points at the end of most chapters. Our mission is to help as many prospective applicants as possible by sharing the knowledge and experience we have gained over the last eight years.

However you choose to use its contents, the main purpose of this book is to help readers gain a basic understanding of what they can expect in the different stages of the admissions process. This step-by-step college planner for students from ninth grade through twelfth grade guides both parent and student through the high school experience. Use this road map in any grade when thinking about college admissions. Do not approach this process with fear and doubt, for by being informed you can face a challenge that can be fun, gratifying, and rewarding. What could be better than shaping your own future? We sincerely wish you the very best in your quest for college admissions.

ONE

College Planner for Students and Parents, Grades Nine through Twelve

In order to learn all about the college admissions process, we have read numerous guides on college admissions, such as *The Fiske Guide to Getting into the Right College, Peterson's Guide to Four-Year Colleges,* and various "how to" guides. After evaluating college catalogs, viewing books, and attending several college information sessions, we realized that there is nothing like going through the admissions process experience ourselves.

We can tell you from personal experience that going through this process for the first time can be intimidating. The biggest mistake we made was not being well informed about the college admissions process. We underestimated the strength of the applicants' academic credentials and the large number of compelling candidates in the applicant pool, both of which make the competition fierce. Had we learned all about the process beforehand, we could have significantly enhanced our son's chances for college admissions.

One of our initial and frightening observations focused on the published information on this process. There is so much information on colleges—an overwhelming volume of material that can be more confusing than helpful. This is a personal account of one who has gone through the experience and has gained a lot by doing so. Over the years we have gained a refined sense of what is necessary and have gleaned useful insights into the college admissions process.

One of the main points that we learned was that a college's admissions committee takes several factors into consideration, including both the academic and personal sides of each applicant. As Marilee Jones, dean of MIT admissions, notes,

> Each applicant is evaluated in two basic ways: objectively and subjectively. The objective evaluation is actually a way of looking at the academic preparation (Grades, rank in class, SAT scores and ranking in relation to that of all

1

other applicants in the pool. . . . The second way we sort each applicant is by the subjective evaluation of the student's application material. Each case is read by at least two different people (admissions staff plus volunteer readers from the faculty and administration) and rated on three specific dimensions of the student's life: initiatives in co-curricular activities; initiatives in interpersonal skills; initiatives in extra-curricular activities (Tse, 6).

In most highly selective colleges, the admissions officers look at six main factors in the admissions process:

1. Academic performance (grades, GPA, and class ranking)
2. Curriculum of challenging courses
3. Standardized test scores
4. College essay
5. Recommendation letters
6. Extracurricular activities (personal qualities)

We will now briefly discuss how one's academic performance and choice of curriculum affect the application process. We will begin to discuss the importance of extracurricular activities; however, this topic, along with standardized test scores, the college essay, and recommendation letters, will be touched upon in great detail in further chapters.

ACADEMIC PERFORMANCE AND CURRICULUM

The admissions officials will look at the applicant's transcripts throughout his or her high school career, starting from the freshman year, and evaluate the following:

1. Courses taken in high school
2. Level of difficulty of these courses (APs and honors)
3. Applicant's academic performance

Most highly selective colleges require four years of English and, depending on the degree of selectivity of the college, from two to four years of mathematics, natural science, social studies, and a foreign language. My children, Vinay and Sheila, signed up for courses that would cover these key subjects. They also made sure to include such basic qualification requirements as health, fine arts, and physical education. We encouraged them to attempt the most challenging courses (the best available) that they could handle. In order to find out what your high school offers, talk to the guidance counselor or look in the school handbook and determine the rigor of the courses. Also, seek advice from your teachers as to which subject level is appropriate for you.

In eleventh grade, Vinay and Sheila made a list of the colleges they were considering. Then they checked all the specific course requirements of these colleges and evaluated their own classes to see if their course selection met all of the requirements. For example, courses that Princeton University recommends applicants take in high school include the following (for the class of 2000):

1. Four years of English
2. Four years of math
3. Four years of the same foreign language
4. Two years of history
5. Two years of laboratory science (Princeton University, 48)

The University of Virginia (UVA), on the other hand, had the following minimum requirements:

1. Four years of English
2. Four years of math
3. One year of social science
4. Two years of science
5. Two years of the same foreign language (University of Virginia, 37)

Most colleges mentioned that these were their minimum requirements, but most successful applicants exceeded this recommendation. Doing so not only makes an applicant a strong candidate in the competitive admissions pool, but exceeding the basic requirements displays evidence of academic motivation and love of learning to the admissions officers, who are always looking for these traits in an applicant. As stated in the 1999–2000 Harvard college guide:

> There is no single academic path we expect all students to follow, but the strongest applicants take the most rigorous secondary school curricula available to them. An ideal four year preparatory program includes four years of English, with extensive practice in writing; four years of math; four years of science: biology, chemistry, physics, and an advanced course in one of these subjects; three years of history, including American and European History; and four years of one foreign language (Harvard University, *Introduction*, 46).

EXTRACURRICULAR ACTIVITIES
(PERSONAL QUALITIES)

We also learned that admissions officers are not simply evaluating students' academic records and test scores. Instead, they also look at other factors, such as extracurricular activities and personal qualifications. We found that admissions officers were not looking for a wide array of extra-curricular activities with no commitment shown; instead, they were look-ing for the candidate's conviction in a few focus areas. A student's com-mitment is usually obvious when he or she puts his or her heart and soul into an activity. Even one extra focus in which the student has made a significant impact in the school, in the community, or on the athletic field can make a difference. Marilee Jones, dean of MIT admissions, assures students that "we do have a tendency to admit students who pursue their activities at a very high level of distinction—regional, state, national, in-ternational level." However, Jones adds, "But the nature of the activities can be anything. It's the passion that counts" (Tse, 6).

Starting in freshman year, we encouraged our kids to explore all the extracurricular activities, such as sports, band, student government, vol-unteer work, and jobs, that were available to them in their school or com-munity. They also explored qualifications required for such associations as the French Society, Math Club, and National Honor Society. They then chose to participate in the extracurricular activities that interested them.

Based on their time and ability to balance these activities with other responsibilities, they eventually narrowed their list of activities to the ones that they really enjoyed. For example, Vinay played several sports, including soccer, basketball, and tennis. As he progressed through high school, he also got involved in volunteer work and organizations such as the Math Club and the French Society. In addition, he was taking more challenging courses. It was difficult maintaining all of these activities without diluting his efforts in academics, so he withdrew his participa-tion in some of the sports and continued with the ones he liked. He really enjoyed tennis and played it in all four years of high school. Since he en-joyed it so much, he was very committed to this activity, which was re-flected in his performance. He was selected as the tennis team's most val-uable player in his senior year.

In contrast, my daughter, Sheila, who had some tennis experience, did not have the same degree of commitment for this sport. Instead, she was very passionate about cross-country running and qualified for the re-gional and state competitions. (She talked about this passion in one of her college essays, included in chapter 11, "The Essay.") The choices made allowed them to express their individuality and to pursue their own inter-ests rather than worrying about becoming the "perfect applicant."

We encouraged Vinay and Sheila to follow their dreams and find their individual passion, yet sometimes both of them liked the same activity. For example, both of them found mock trial interesting and pursued it for four years; they were both team captains in their senior year. We made sure that they had a sincere interest and were committed for at least two to four years to each activity.

To demonstrate this commitment, my children created an activity journal, where they recorded all of the activities in which they participated—dates, hours per week, a brief explanation, leadership positions, and awards and accomplishments. This information was very useful later when it was time to complete their college applications. They also had plenty of time for an active social life consisting of football games, school dances, and sleepovers. This variety enabled them to have a complete high school experience. We felt that what they made of their high school experience was as important as where they attended college. In summation, we felt that students should have a healthy balance between their academic pursuits, extracurricular activities, and social lives.

COLLEGE PLANNER TIPS FOR GRADES NINE THROUGH TWELVE

Ninth Grade

As freshmen in high school, students are immature and can easily be distracted by the whole high school experience. They may be easily tempted to dilute their efforts toward academic performance with other social activities. We reminded our kids to stay focused and to have a sense of direction from the beginning of their high school careers. When students slack off and get poor grades, they will eventually undermine their class ranking.

SEPTEMBER

1. Make an appointment with the school counselor as early as your freshman year.
2. Use the school's course listings to outline a comprehensive academic plan for the next four years of high school.
3. Plan to cover all the key subjects: English, science, history, mathematics, and foreign language.
4. Make sure to include all of the school's basic requirement courses, such as health, fine arts, and physical education needed to graduate from high school.
5. Determine what course levels are appropriate for you.
6. Ask yourself if you are comfortable with the academic challenge.
7. Plan to take the appropriate prerequisites needed for the advanced placement (AP) courses in the future.

8. Set high standards by setting goals to get good grades and take challenging courses.
9. Envision what you want your transcript to look like.
10. Plan your extracurricular activities.

SUMMER

1. Begin résumé-enhancing activities that are worthwhile and that you will enjoy for the summer. Examples might include summer camp, travel, volunteer work, and summer programs.
2. Have a summer reading list.
3. Build your SAT vocabulary.

Tenth Grade

SEPTEMBER

1. Outline and establish goals for your sophomore year.
2. Determine what classes you need to take.
3. Take as many challenging courses as you can possibly handle.
4. Evaluate your previous coursework to establish if you have fulfilled all of the qualification requirements for important courses in your junior and senior year.
5. Ask yourself if you are maintaining your grades. Focus on your academic performance.
6. Evaluate in what extracurricular activities you wish to remain involved.
7. Ask yourself if you have explored all of the extracurricular activities that are available.
8. Decide which activity most interests you.
9. Inquire at your guidance office about any college fairs in your area and plan to attend them.
10. Plan to take the SAT II test in May or June, if appropriate. Since the test is based on academic subjects that you have probably already completed, the best time to take it is at the end of the most relevant subject. (See chapter 2, "Standardized Tests," for details.)
11. Sign up for a practice PSAT/NMSQT, offered to sophomore students in October. According to the College Board's website on the PSAT, www.sat-acttestprep.com/psat.htm, "the PSAT is the Preliminary Scholastic Assessment Test. It is a two-hour test given once a year in October. There are five separate sections: two math sections, two verbal sections, and one writing skills section. Each subject is scored on a scale from 20 to 80 points for a total of 240 maxi-

mum points. National Merit Scholarship semifinalists are selected based on the PSAT score." Most high school students take the PSAT during their junior year. However, many schools now allow sophomores to take the test for practice (College Board).

OCTOBER

1. Plan to take your practice PSAT/NMSQT.

MARCH

1. Register for May SAT II.
2. If you are planning to take the SAT II exams, you may consider buying a preparation guide from publishers such as Barron's, Kaplan, or The Princeton Review. These guides do not teach you everything you need to know about the subject, but they focus on useful techniques for scoring well. Practice tests help students prepare for the real test. In addition, it helps them to become familiar with the test format and have fewer surprises on the exam day. Our kids evaluated their strong subjects and planned to take SAT II tests in those subjects in May and/or June.

APRIL

1. Register for June SAT II.

MAY–JUNE

1. Take the SAT II tests in the major subjects in which you have excelled (May/June dates).

SUMMER

1. Improve your test-taking skills if you get a low score on the practice, PSAT, test. Consider taking the preparation courses to strengthen your skills. There are several test preparation guides such as those from The Princeton Review, ARCO, and Kaplan. These guides include helpful material such as diagnostic tests, sample tests with answers and explanations, and tips on test-taking tactics, all of which help users raise their test scores. The College Board publishes *10 Real SATs*. The real practice helped my kids familiarize themselves with the test format and perform their best on the SAT test.

2. Identify constructive programs in which you can be involved this
   summer.
3. Have a summer reading list. *Read! Read! Read!*
4. Browse college magazines and guides. Explore the Internet for information.
5. Evaluate the strengths and weaknesses of your academic performance and extracurricular achievements.
6. Keep track of all the SAT I, II, and ACT test dates. Look through
   and plan as to which months are most suitable for you to take the
   tests in eleventh grade.

Eleventh Grade

This was one of the most challenging years for my kids. This is the crucial year for standardized testing. They had their PSAT, AP, SAT II, and
SAT I testing all within a brief amount of time. My daughter was lucky
that she was able to successfully complete some of the SAT II in tenth
grade. My son, on the other hand, took all the tests after the eleventh
grade and had a very small sample of SAT II scores from which to choose.
In addition, they had attained seniority positions in some of their activities as their teams lost a lot of older players with the graduating class.
They also achieved leadership roles in some clubs for the same reason.
All of these changes meant more responsibility and significant commitment and dedication to their involvement. Both of my kids were also taking a lot of challenging courses such as honors, AP, and college courses
during their junior year. This course load was a lot more intense than in
their previous years. They also had to focus on the best possible academic
performance. To combat the weight of these stresses, give your kids as
much positive feedback as possible. Make sure they have their own leisure time and maintain a healthy balance between work and play. We encouraged our kids to invite their friends over for dinner, to have sleepovers, to go to school games and dances, and to participate in weekend
family vacations.

SEPTEMBER

1. Make a list of colleges that interest you. Look through college view
   books, catalogs, and similar publications. Visit the colleges' home
   pages on the Internet. Read all of the information thoroughly.
2. Review your high school courses for the next two years. Take as
   many challenging courses (APs and honors) as you can handle.
   Highly selective colleges closely examine if you are taking more

challenging courses in the progressive years and if your performance is improving (or if you are slacking off).

3. Do you have a strong academic record? Set goals to achieve the highest grades possible.
4. Evaluate if all of your courses meet the admissions requirement.
5. Keep track of all the courses needed for your graduation requirement.
6. Evaluate and analyze all of the strengths and weaknesses in your extracurricular activities. Cut down and tailor a set of activities that are the most meaningful to you. Show signs of initiative and leadership in these activities.
7. Do your academic profile and activities reflect the true impressions you want to make on the admissions committee?
8. Register to take the PSAT test.
9. Check with your guidance counselor for a list of college fairs in the area and plan to attend with your parents. Get information on the college and sign up to be on their mailing list.
10. Inquire about the college representatives visiting the school and plan to attend their information sessions. You will get an insight as to what kind of test scores and grades you will need in order to fulfill their admissions requirement.

OCTOBER

1. Plan to take the PSAT test. Your PSAT test score will determine whether you qualify for the National Merit Scholarship. This test also prepares you for the SAT exams that you will be taking later.
2. Visit colleges, if convenient.
3. Look up all of the SAT II and I test dates available in November, December, January, May, and June. In March, only SAT I is offered. Plan to take these tests.
4. Review and identify all of the test dates that most suit you. Check the deadlines for registrations. Parent and student should make an appointment with the guidance counselor to finalize all of the appropriate dates to take these tests in eleventh grade.
5. Keep track of all the registration deadlines and test dates on your calendar.

DECEMBER

1. Review your test PSAT scores. If you received low scores, consider taking preparatory courses to strengthen your skills before you attempt the SAT in spring or earlier.

2. Plan to schedule college visits in the spring. Check with the colleges if they can arrange an overnight stay for you.
3. Check all of the test dates and registration deadlines.

MARCH

1. Review your test dates and registration deadlines.
2. Plan to visit colleges during your spring break. Plan to stay overnight if appropriate. This way you can see the campus in full swing and not miss school.

MAY

1. Take the appropriate advanced placement exams.
2. Look up SAT and ACT test dates and registration deadlines.

SUMMER

1. Look through the college catalogs and decide on the college or university to which you would like to apply this year.
2. Consider planning college visits in summer or fall. A campus visit can provide an excellent introduction to the actual college setting.
3. If you plan to have a campus interview, you should notify the college well in advance (at least three weeks).
4. Write letters to the colleges to request an application and any supplementary information.
5. Draft your résumé.
6. Record all of your extracurricular activities by making an activity chart.
7. Update your volunteer work and make a chart.
8. Review and update all of your academic records.
9. Record all of your awards and honors.
10. Work on your college essay topics.
11. Start working on the college applications that you received.
12. Focus on a few teachers that you wish to consider asking for recommendation letters for your college applications.
13. Have a goal to fulfill all of the test requirements by October if applying for early admission and by November if applying for regular admission.
14. Continue your involvement in summer activities.

Twelfth Grade

Balancing the application process with schoolwork, activities, and other responsibilities might seem like lot of work and can be an overwhelming experience, but it is all worth the effort once you get admitted to a college of your choice. Fall of senior year is a very busy time for students. Not only did our kids have all of the college essays and applications to complete, they also had to keep up with their schoolwork and maintain grades. In addition, they had to balance all of their extracurricular activities, sports, volunteer work, school games, and dances. We reminded and encouraged them to stay focused and set their priorities because they would have plenty of time to have fun later in the year when all of this was over. By concentrating on what was important, they had the satisfaction of giving their schoolwork and applications their best shot and not fretting about it later.

SEPTEMBER

1. *Finalize* your target list of colleges to which you want to apply.
2. Evaluate all of the outstanding tests that you require for college admission. Establish goals and set target dates to complete these tests.
3. Evaluate if these test dates fall within the admissions requirement of the colleges to which you wish to apply.
4. Check with the guidance office as to the college fairs in your area and if any college admissions representatives are visiting your school. Plan to go prepared with some questions that genuinely concern you.
5. Plan college visits and set up a campus interview, if convenient. Check with each college regarding the deadline for college interviews. In my experience, most colleges conducted college interviews through December. The interview appointment slots get filled up fast, so *call early*!
6. You may want to revise and update your college list based on your impressions and information that you get from these college visits. You may want to change your mind as to which college to apply early. (See chapter 6 on college visits for details.)
7. Make sure that you have received all of the necessary college applications.
8. Start working on your college essays and applications. Set goals to complete the early decision/action applications by a certain date and work toward fulfilling these goals.
9. Ask your teachers for letters of recommendation.
10. Ask your guidance counselor or principal for letters of recommendation.
11. Admissions officers look at the courses that you take and the grades that you get in your senior year. A consistent and full transcript is impressive.

12. Set goals to get good grades in order to have the best possible GPA and class ranking. Pursue the goal that is attainable for you.
13. Consider taking some college courses in your junior or senior year.

1. Follow up on all of the requested recommendations.
2. Take SAT II or I (or ACT), if necessary.
3. Plan and finalize if you wish to apply for early decision or for early action. Review all of your options.
4. Start working on fulfilling some of the application requirements, especially those for early decision and early action.
5. Get an English teacher or parent to proofread your essay. Finalize some of your essays.
6. Make a master test score chart to record the following:
   - Test names
   - Test dates
   - Test scores
   - Reminders to release the appropriate test scores to the colleges
   (See chapter 8 on applications for details.)
7. Make folders for each college and on each cover of the folder make a chart and record the following (my daughter was the originator of this plan):
   - All of the parts of the application (part I and part II)
   - Teacher recommendation forms (form 1 and form 2)
   - Counselor's recommendations and school transcripts
   - Application fees
   - Test scores
   - Midterm reports
   Sheila also made check boxes and marked the ones that were processed.
   (See chapter 8 on applications for details.)
8. Make a list of all of the teachers to which you gave the letters of recommendation forms. Note the date submitted and the form title (Example: "Teacher A" or "Form 1") and the corresponding colleges. This is very important because all of the colleges have different titles for these recommendation forms, and if one of your teachers misplaces a form it will be easy to trace if you have that information on record. Teachers will be getting piles of letters of recommendation requests, and misplacing one of them is quite possible. Also, chances are colleges may not receive all of the recommendations. If this happens to you, all you will have to do is call the appropriate college and request a new application. These few

simple planning and organizing tips save a lot of time and anguish when you, your teacher, or the college misplaces the recommendation form. (See chapter 12 on recommendation letters for details.)

9. Follow the same procedure for guidance letters of recommendation.
10. Make a master list on which you record information needed for all the colleges:
    - College names and their application deadlines
    - Application fees
    - Test scores to be released to different colleges
    - Recommendation letters
    - Dates when recommendations were submitted or mailed
    - All the completed applications and mailing dates.

NOVEMBER

1. You may start receiving calls for alumni interviews. Be prepared. (See chapter 7 on interviews for details.)
2. Prepare for SAT and ACT tests, if needed.
3. Alert yourself to the early application deadlines.
4. Work toward completion of some college applications.
5. Keep up with your schoolwork and activities.
6. Promptly mail all of the completed applications.
7. Two weeks after you have mailed any application, call the college and inquire if your application is complete and if they have received all of the parts.

DECEMBER

1. Most selective colleges have their application deadlines on the first of the year, so check all of your application deadlines.
2. Check to see if your high school has mailed all of the necessary information, such as recommendations and transcripts, to all of your perspective colleges.

FEBRUARY

1. Check to see if you have submitted all midterm reports to the guidance office and that the school has mailed them to the appropriate colleges before their deadline.
2. Apply for scholarships and awards.

APRIL

1. Finalize your decision on the college or university that you wish to attend this fall.
2. Inform the college or university about your decision to accept.
3. If you are on a waiting list, mail the card back with your reply. (See chapter 15 on waiting lists for details.)

MAY

1. *Congratulations!*
2. See the appendix, "College Supply List," on what to pack for college.
3. Take AP test(s), if appropriate.

COURSE SELECTION CHART FOR HIGH SCHOOL

Ninth Grade

1. _____
2. _____
3. _____
4. _____
5. _____
6. _____
7. _____

Tenth Grade

1. _____
2. _____
3. _____
4. _____
5. _____
6. _____
7. _____

Eleventh Grade

1. _____
2. _____
3. _____
4. _____
5. _____
6. _____
7. _____

Twelfth Grade

1. _____
2. _____
3. _____
4. _____
5. _____
6. _____
7. _____

1. Look up each year in your school handbook.
2. Make sure to include all of the basic courses that are required by your school in order to graduate.
3. Include all of the courses that would cover the subjects in all the key areas such as English, science, history, mathematics, and foreign language.
4. Consider taking challenging courses progressively. Consider including AP and honor courses, especially in your junior and senior year.
5. Consider taking some college courses in the summer or during the school year.

Two

Standardized Tests

Test scores are one of several factors that help colleges make admissions decisions. Most highly selective colleges require prospective students to take the Scholastic Assessment Test (SAT I) and Subject Tests, formerly known as Achievement Tests (SAT II) (in three different subjects) or the American College Test (ACT) test before the application deadline. You should review all of your college catalogs to find out the specific requirements for each institution. Colleges use these test scores to compare the applicant with other candidates with diverse backgrounds, preparatory experience, and grade averages. The SAT test score is a standardized way of holistically measuring an applicant's capabilities for handling college-level work. In contrast, SAT II scores can give an admissions officer a reliable assessment of an applicant's academic strength in a particular subject. Together these tests can provide an admissions officer with a more complete picture of the student's academic profile.

In order to address this major element of the admissions process, outline all of the test dates and plan ahead to take these tests throughout your high school career. You can register for these tests on-line by visiting www.collegeboard.org or by mail by writing to:

College Board SAT Program
P.O. Box 6200
Princeton, NJ 08541-6200

If you have registered as a high school student for an earlier SAT II or I test, you may also re-register by phone: 1-609-771-7600.

Make sure to register for your SAT I test before the deadline to avoid a late fee. Deadline dates for registration are usually five weeks before the exam, whereas late registration deadlines are three weeks before the exam. Check with your high school guidance office for details. When registering for these tests, you will need to supply valid information, including:

1. Your full name
2. Your social security number
3. Your high school code (code of the school you are currently attending)
4. Test center code (code of the center where you are planning to take the test)

You will also need to ascertain the registration fees for each test. The SAT I and SAT II are offered simultaneously, and either can be taken on any date except for the testing date in March, which is exclusively for the SAT I.

THE SAT II

Why Take SAT II Tests?

In addition to the SAT I, most highly selective colleges require students to take the SAT II in three subject areas, usually in writing, math, and a subject area of their choice. (See below for complete list of tests offered.) Check with the colleges to which you are applying for what and how many SAT II tests are required. No matter what your school (public, private, preparatory) or background, the SAT II serves as a way for colleges to compare different students on the same level.

When to Take the SAT II

The key factor to doing your best on the SAT II is timing. Since the test is based on academic subjects, the ideal time to take the SAT II is either in May or June when you complete the relevant subject course, whether you are in ninth, tenth, or eleventh grade. This way, the subject material is fresh in your mind. My daughter, for example, took the SAT II in chemistry soon after she took a chemistry honors class in tenth grade. She withheld the scores and knew that she had plenty of time to retake this test, if necessary. Surprisingly, she did well and therefore had one fewer test to worry about. Taking tests early and after completing the respective courses in school allowed her to get a head start. While we encouraged our kids to take the SAT II tests as early as possible, we felt it was advisable to take the SAT II in writing as late as possible because students' writing skills improve as they progress through high school.

The best strategy is not to take too many tests at one time—Instead, spread tests out in order to achieve your optimal performance. Start taking tests as early as freshman year; by starting early, you will have the opportunity to retake the test if you feel that your scores do not accurately reflect your aptitude. In addition, you may choose to take an extra course in a subject if your test score was low. Sometimes the best approach is to take the AP tests in conjunction with the SAT II subject tests. With this combined testing, the student can prepare for both exams in depth.

Score Choice

In fall 2002, the College Board eliminated the score choice option for Sat II subject tests. For application purposes, all colleges and universities will consider only a student's highest SAT II scores. For more information, visit the College Board website at www.collegeboard.com.

Evaluating Your Score

SAT II tests are scored on a scale of 200–800. In my experience, a high score on a SAT II test (scores above 650, depending on the subjects and on college choice) indicates a mastery of subject area. Since SAT II tests are based on a specific subject, the higher the SAT II test scores, the higher the credibility given to that course in your high school.

SAT II Subject Tests Offered

Writing	Chinese
Literature	French
American History and Social Studies	German
World History	Modern Hebrew
Math Level IC	Italian
Math Level IIC	Japanese
Biology	Latin
Chemistry	Spanish
Physics	English Language Proficiency

When registering for SAT II, students must specify the particular subject test. Each exam is a one-hour comprehensive test that evaluates student's skills within that subject. Students may take one, two, or three tests at the most on a given test date and registration fees will vary accordingly. However, if you change your mind about taking more than one subject test on the test date, you may do so. For example, my daughter registered to take the SAT II in English only, yet on the test date she changed her mind and felt confident enough to attempt the SAT II exam in math as well. She was later billed for the additional test.

THE SAT I

The SAT I is three times as long as the SAT II, lasting three hours. It tests verbal and math skills. There are three separate test sections in each category. In addition, the test contains an experimental section, which could be either in math or verbal, making a total of seven sections in each test. Test scores range from 200 to 800 in each category of verbal and math, for a total score of 1,600. Read all the directions on the test ahead of time, so that on the actual test you do not waste time reading the directions and panic. An excerpted list from Kaplan's *The Road to College* advises students to "remember that a little anxiety is natural. Managing your adrenaline and the ability to focus are key elements of success on standardized tests—and in admissions process."

High-achieving students do not necessarily get good standardized test scores. Sometimes students with average school grades have excellent SAT scores. These results may occur because they were naturally brilliant, risk takers, or just lucky. However, one definitely must master the art of test taking in order to perform well on these standardized tests, regardless of native intelligence or a history of good grades. As Stanley Kaplan, founder of Kaplan Educational Centers, says, "No one would enter a tennis tournament without ever having held a tennis racquet. You must learn, then practice, practice, practice. And no student should ever, ever take a college entrance exam without taking a sample exam. There is only one way to build up your test-taking skills: to be familiar with the directions, the timing, and the content of the test—and then practice, practice, practice"(Nieuwenhuis, 154).

My own experiences illustrate the necessity of honing these skills. When my kids took some of their first sample tests without practice, their scores were average, providing no outstanding scores for highly selective colleges. They then bought guides from the College Board, Barron's, and The Princeton Review. These guides included helpful material such as diagnostic tests, sample tests with answers and explanations, and tips on test-taking tactics, all of which help users raise test scores. In addition, my children took SAT preparatory courses (Kaplan/Princeton Review) for one session to help them with test-taking strategies. In these courses, instructors give students some practice tests, timing them and simulating the actual test atmosphere. They then analyze their performance and give students personalized feedback, pointing out their strengths and weaknesses.

Not only did this preparation help my children familiarize themselves with the test format, it also improved their test-taking skills. As a result, their scores improved as much as 200 to 300 points from the first SAT sample test, taken in the summer after tenth grade. In addition, there is a big difference in kids' maturity level between tenth and eleventh grade. By eleventh grade, they are, after all, more serious about going to college, and this change is also reflected in their test performance.

The verbal section of the SAT I consists of reading comprehension, sentence completions, and analogies. Overall, verbal sections test your reading skills, determining how well you think, reason, and process the context in the passage. If a student is a voracious reader, he or she has an advantage and will do well in this part of the test. Students' performance on the verbal section of the SAT I will most likely improve throughout their high school years, I did notice a significant improvement in my children's verbal scores when comparing tests taken in fall and spring of eleventh grade, respectively. Besides their having a better grasp of English in progressive years, one of the other reasons for improvement in these standardized tests is the fact that my children had more in-depth knowledge of history and science; with that background they could more effectively tackle the SAT I reading comprehension questions dealing with these subjects.

To do well on the verbal section, one should have a firm grasp of two areas: reading comprehension and vocabulary. The best strategy to improve your score is vocabulary memorization. Vinay and Sheila made flash cards of unfamiliar words and then repeatedly referred to them until they had learned them. The best approach to improve your score is preparation. Get familiar with the words and definitions by reviewing them as often as you eat.

For the math section of the SAT I, a solid background including arithmetic, algebra, and geometry courses is all that is helpful, for the test does not ask questions beyond these categories. And again, the best preparation is practice, practice, and more practice. An Olympic swimmer who has not practiced for a while can quickly lose his or her endurance. Only with practice and training can the athlete build his or her resilience. So too, in math, practice is the best approach. With practice, my kids were able to sharpen their skills, acquainting themselves with some of the most commonly asked questions. They knew the best strategies, such as how to pace themselves, how not to spend too much time on one problem, and when to guess and when to move on. With these tips, they were less intimidated by the trickier questions.

With this experience and advice in mind, do not despair if you do not do well the first time, for there is plenty of time for improvement. However, start this process early. My son waited until the spring of eleventh grade to take all of the standardized tests. Not only did he have to take all of his tests at once, but he also had fewer score options from which to choose. When he attempted one of the SAT II tests, he was very ill and did not give his best effort. In addition, since he started testing so late in the spring, he was running out of dates to retake tests before the application deadline. While starting early for SAT II exams is highly encouraged because the ideal time is when you complete the relevant subject, you do not want to take the SAT I prematurely. If my kids had to do it again, I would have them wait until junior year (either fall or spring, depending on how comfortable and well prepared they were) to attempt the SAT I for the first time. From our experience, SAT I scores earned in eleventh grade showed drastic improvement over those from tenth grade. However, there are many advantages to completing SAT I and SAT II test taking by the end of eleventh grade, as mentioned later in this chapter.

Your test scores are mailed to you three weeks after you take the test. For an additional charge, scores are also available in two weeks by phone. The toll-free number is 1-800-728-7267.

THE ACT

In contrast to the SAT, which has a math and a verbal section, the ACT has four categories: English, reading, math, and science. The ACT tests are based on high school curricula. While the SAT is designed to assess your ability to do college-level work, the ACT, on the other hand, measures your knowledge of a particular subject and hence some students prefer the ACT to the SAT. One of the reasons may be the fact that the ACT has only a 25 percent math section compared to the 50 percent math section of the SAT. If math is not your strong subject, you may want to take this fact into consideration. Another fact to consider is that the ACT has a 25 percent science subject area compared to the SAT, which does not have any section on science. Finally, for most colleges that accept the ACT, the test replaces both the SAT I and SAT II tests. Experience suggests that if you are a better test taker, the SAT may be a better option, and if you are good at schoolwork/homework and get good grades, then the ACT may be a possible better option. The ACT test consists of 215 multiple-choice questions and lasts for three and one-half hours (including a break time of half an hour). Most students take the ACT twice, once in their junior year and once in their senior year. ACT tests and SAT I are administered seven times a year.

What ACT Scores Are Released if Students Test More Than Once?

As noted on the ACT website (www.act.org/aap/faq/general.html), for students who are considering taking the test more than once, the ACT assures the release of scores for requested dates only. This protects and guarantees students that they retain control of their records. The organization creates records for each specific test date. Students may report multiple scores to a college. However, ACT, Inc. will not compile an average of these scores to be sent to the desired institution (ACT, Inc).

SEEKING OUTSIDE HELP

There are several prep courses available for the standardized tests.

1. Kaplan Educational Centers: www.kaplan.com; 1-800-kap-test
2. The Princeton Review: www.review.com; 1-800-2-review
3. Stanford Testing Systems: www.prep.com
4. Prep Doctor: www.prepdoctor.com

ADVANTAGES TO COMPLETING TESTING
BY YOUR JUNIOR YEAR

1. You will probably have all of your test scores and other information in time to help you plan early for college admissions.
2. You will have the test score information about yourself and the admission requirements of the college you are interested in before your campus visit, making your visits more meaningful since you will know whether your test scores fall within the range of admitted students.
3. Colleges will have all your test scores in time. In addition, they will know about your interest and academic skills before the senior year, when many colleges send admissions information to potential candidates.
4. By jump-starting this process, you may be able to fulfill all of your test requirements before your senior year. This could give you an added advantage over the other applicants and help you come across as organized and well prepared.
5. You will have the option to retest in the fall of your senior year if you feel that your score did not precisely portray your aptitude.

TIPS FOR PARENTS

In large public schools, due to funding cutbacks, students may not have access to all of the information and advice needed to guide them through the admission process. Thus, parents and students should take an active role in this process. Ideally, you should start as early as your child's fresh-

man year. Students should make an appointment with the school counselor and sketch out a comprehensive academic plan that includes
courses that they will be taking for the next four years of their high school
careers. Then parents and kids should sit down and plan as to which date,
month, and year to take the SAT I and SAT II subject test and/or the ACT.
With this strategic plan, the student is not stressed by packing too many
tests into too little time before the application deadline in his or her senior
year.

Keep in mind:

1. These test dates may not always work as planned.
2. These dates might clash with students' midterm exams, school activities, and very crucial regional/state sports playoffs.
3. Problems such as misreading test directions may occur; so additional test dates might be necessary.
4. Due to physical illness, students may not be able to take the test.
5. Students may not be satisfied with the test score results and may
   want to retake these tests.
6. You may need to look ahead for plenty of backup dates where your
   kids can retake these tests before the college application deadline.

IMPORTANT POINTS TO REMEMBER

1. Almost all highly selective colleges need applicants to have at least
   three SAT II achievement test scores and the SAT I or ACT.
2. These test scores give the admission officers a standardized way of
   assessing all the various applicants' capabilities since each student
   has a different background.
3. Check with all of the colleges to which you wish to apply about
   their specific test requirements for admissions.
4. Plan ahead to take these tests and keep track of registration deadlines.
5. Consider buying some study guides to help you improve your test
   scores.
6. Practice on some sample tests and review your strengths and weaknesses.
7. Consider taking some preparation course such as The Princeton Review or Kaplan, if needed.
8. Remember that on these test dates, students can either take up to
   three SAT IIs at a time or the SAT I (except in March, when only the
   SAT I is offered).
9. The best strategy is not to crowd too many SAT II subject tests at

one time. Your preparation for these tests may be diluted and your scores may not accurately reflect your capability.

10. The key element in doing your best on the SAT II subject tests is timing. Students should try to take these tests as early as tenth or even ninth grade, for the reasons explained above.

THREE

Advanced Placement Testing and Courses

One of the many factors considered in the admissions process is the level of difficulty of a student's course selection. Most highly selective colleges want students to take the most challenging courses possible. Although advanced placement (AP) courses are not required for admissions, taking high-level courses greatly improves your chances of acceptance. As noted by The Princeton Review, "College admissions officers are more favorably disposed to students who take AP courses" (Meltzer, 4).

The inclusion of AP courses can strengthen a transcript. Taking AP courses indicates to admissions officers that the applicant is academically motivated. Keep in mind, however, that AP courses are the hardest courses offered in high school. They usually involve more work than other classes and most often have tougher exams. For these reasons, taking AP courses may result in lower grades. But consider on the other hand the fact that "many admissions officers will give your AP grade a one-level 'bump.' That is, they will consider your 'C' as a 'B' " (Meltzer, 4).

When considering which courses to take, note that the College Board coordinates all of the AP programs and administers the college admissions examinations that are taken after the completion of the AP course; attaining a certain score may provide you college credit. The organization offers over thirty college-level courses in eighteen subject areas. Each AP exam is based on the coursework outlined in its respective subject. Most exams are three hours long, but some subject tests may be longer or shorter. Check with AP literature for specific details. Exams are administered in May at the end of the school year. Tests are given in the morning or afternoon, depending on the subject. AP tests are scored on a scale of 1 to 5, with 5 being the highest. As noted in the College Board's *Advanced Placement Program Bulletin for Students and Parents*, the rating system is as follows: 5 = extremely well qualified; 4 = well qualified; 3 = qualified; 2 = possibly qualified; and 1 = no recommendation (13).

If you are planning to take an AP exam, you should talk to your guidance counselor in January and register before the deadline, which usually falls around March 1. Your scores will be released to you around mid-July. To find out more about AP tests, try any or all of the following methods:

1. Talk to your guidance counselor.
2. Write to the College Board at:
   AP Services
   P.O. Box 6671
   Princeton, NJ 08541-6671.
3. Telephone the College Board at 1-609-771-7300 or call toll-free at 1-888-225-5427.
4. E-mail to apexam@ets.org.
5. Visit the College Board's website at *www.collegeboard.org/ap.*.

In addition to providing college credit, a good AP score is impressive and can definitely enhance your application. While both AP and SAT II subject test scores evaluate a student's performance in similar subjects, it is often to your advantage to take both the AP exam and the SAT II in a certain subject, especially if you have a mediocre or low SAT II score. For example, a SAT II score of 600 is good but not considered a standout performance in highly selective colleges (See chapter 2 for details). AP scores used in conjunction with SAT II scores and your high school transcript give an admissions officer a reliable measure of your academic strength. Exceptional AP scores can surely complement average SAT II scores and boost your application profile. According to admissions officer Michele A. Hernández in *A Is for Admission:* "An SAT II score of 670 on the biology exam is strong, although not exceptional in the Ivy pool. But the 5 on the AP exam represents a strong grasp of college-level biology . . . high AP scores could suddenly change the picture dramatically" (92). Furthermore, AP courses taken in your senior year definitely improve your application since they add strength to your curriculum. However, it is too late for any remarkable scores to be considered for the admissions process since they are released in July. You can pursue taking an AP course in a subject area of interest to you. Consider taking as many AP courses as you can comfortably handle.

VINAY AND SHEILA'S EXPERIENCE

Vinay and Sheila: At our high school, most AP courses were offered to juniors and seniors. Sophomore students had a limited choice of AP courses. In most cases, students had to fulfill certain requirements and prerequisites before taking an AP course. For this reason, we had to wait until junior year before becoming eligible to take certain AP courses. Check with your school catalog for details about your individual school's policies regarding AP courses. At our school, we were able to take our first AP course as early as our sophomore year. We accordingly took the AP exam at the end of the year upon completion of the course. Not only were we able to give our best when taking the exam because the subject material was fresh in our minds, but completing one AP exam at the end of sophomore year saved us the agony of waiting until the end of junior year to take all of our tests at one time.

In order to prepare for the AP exams, we took certain key steps. First, we bought some preparation guides, such as The Princeton Review or Barron's, which helped us to familiarize ourselves with the test format. We made sure to buy these guides at the beginning of the year, but we really started referring to them about three months before the test two to three times a week for a span of about one hour. We reviewed more frequently as the test date approached. We also took some practice tests that were either in the guidebooks we purchased or were copies of previous years' exams, which our teacher provided. One can also purchase past exams through the College Board for further practice. Taking and retaking practice exams helped us assess our strengths and weaknesses and hence helped us prepare for the exams. We each attempted over seven AP courses throughout our high school careers, although we approached them in different ways.

Sheila: I took only a few of these AP exams. Once I found out that I was admitted to Harvard early decision and learned that the college did not award credit for AP scores, I still took many AP courses, but I decided not to attempt all of the AP exams during my senior year. Instead of awarding college credit, Harvard offers advanced standing. If enough AP exams are taken in which a student receives a high score (a 4 or 5), advanced standing is granted, whereby a student can, for example, graduate early.

Vinay: I, on the other hand, got college credit for any AP score of 5 at MIT and advanced placement in that subject for a score of 4. This means that if I scored a 4 or above, I could take a higher-level course in that specific subject area. Because I had earned numerous college credits from my AP scores while still in high school, I was able to graduate from MIT with both a major and a minor, which would have been an extremely difficult task to accomplish in four years considering the challenging curriculum at MIT. Another option I had was to earn a double major in four years by writing a thesis. All of these options are easier to achieve with college credit from AP scores.

Keep in mind that each college has a different approach to its awarding of college credit from AP scores. You should, therefore, find out from the prospective colleges their individual policies concerning credit for AP exams. AP policies are usually printed in the college course catalog. You can also write or call an admissions officer of a college for further details about the policies.

It is also important to remember that you do not have to take AP courses to take the AP exams. Preparing for AP exams on your own requires tremendous discipline, self-motivation, and the ability to teach yourself an intricate AP course load, but the payoffs are great. One student I knew at MIT had taken twelve AP exams when he was in high school. He took many of the exams without having taken the respective subjects in high school. This allowed him to skip a year in college. It costs around $75 to take each AP exam. It may seem a steep price to pay, but considering the fact that students can get college credit for each course, it usually works out economically in the long run. Tuition for one year at a private school is roughly $28,000. In addition, AP courses help students build the proficiency that they will need in college.

Vinay and Sheila: We have prepared the following information and tips based on our own experiences. Much of this advice was definitely learned by going through this process as high school students and gaining hindsight from this experience.

What Should I Do to Prepare Myself without Appearing Too Preprogrammed?

1. Take the hardest course load you can handle.
2. Complete electives in your first year. This way you can take challenging courses (AP/honors) in your eleventh and twelfth grades that may not have been offered to you as a freshman.
3. Take harder classes progressively.
4. Take at least five or more honors or AP courses, especially in eleventh and twelfth grades. Remember an AP course load is very heavy and intense.
5. Keep in mind that colleges look at the transcript and see what was offered in your school (level of difficulty of courses, choice of classes) and how well you took advantage of the most challenging curriculum choices.

How Important Are Grades?

1. Try to maintain an A or B average; avoid having C's on your transcript.
2. The more highly selective/competitive the college, the more good grades and a high GPA become important.

3. Good AP grades can positively add to your applications to increase your chances for admission to highly selective colleges.
4. High AP scores on AP exams can earn you college credit.

What Kinds of Awards Are Offered for AP Performance?

The College Board awards AP scholar recognition, which is granted to all students who receive a 3 or higher on three or more AP exams on full-year courses. This award adds to your résumé and academic profile. In addition, more prestigious awards are given to students who have taken more AP courses and earned higher grades. These awards are mentioned on your AP score report, which is mailed to your prospective colleges.

How Can I Use My Scores to My Advantage? Can I Cancel and Withhold Scores?

Most colleges and universities grant credit for high scores (3 or higher) received on an AP exam; others offer advanced standing. Each school's score requirement for the eligibility of college credit or advanced placement is different. Call or write to the individual college to find out its specific policy. Regardless of whether you get AP credit, admissions officers are impressed when you are taking AP courses and it adds to your academic profile favorably.

According to the College Board's *Advanced Placement Program Bulletin*, if you have concerns about poor performance on an AP exam you have until June 15 of the year you take the test to decide if you want to cancel your scores. There is no fee, but this option does require a signature to be processed. If you do not opt for this choice and you receive a low score on an AP test, you may decide to withhold your scores. A score of 1 or 2 may be viewed unfavorably, especially if you received A's in that class. This performance may create doubts in the minds of admissions officers as to the quality of your school, classes, and curriculum (by comparing them to national standards). You therefore have the option of holding back your AP scores if your scores are low. By writing to the AP program and identifying the AP exam, the date taken, your personal information, including full name and home address, and the name, city, and state of the colleges you would like not to receive your scores, you can hold back your scores. This process requires a fee of approximately $5 (College Board, 14).

What Do I Need to Know about These Tests?

1. Most AP exams are taken in May.
2. AP tests are offered in a broad range of subjects including English,

French, Spanish, chemistry, biology, physics, government and politics, calculus AB, calculus BC, U.S. history, and European history.

3. You can take AP tests without having taken the course, but it requires an immense amount of studying on the individual's part.

4. Familiarize yourself with the exam format before the test date; it is beneficial to purchase a guidebook in the corresponding subject area in which you plan to take the test and use it as a reference throughout the school year.

5. While most SAT II tests are one hour long and consist of multiple-choice questions, most AP exams are three hours long and include two sections: multiple choice and free response. According to the *Advanced Placement Program Bulletin*: "Free-response questions require you to organize your knowledge and to produce clear, coherent answers that demonstrate your understanding of the discipline and of special concepts. These answers can take the form of essay, solutions to problems, or programs" (College Board, 4).

6. AP tests do not substitute for SAT II tests.

7. College credits are not granted for SAT II subject tests.

8. High AP scores can complement mediocre SAT II scores.

9. AP scores can give better insight into a student's academic strengths and weaknesses.

10. Remember that only the scores of AP tests taken before twelfth grade will be considered in the college application process since the exam is taken in May at the end of the school year.

11. A heavy course load including many AP's enhances your application.

How Does Grade Reporting Work?

1. Grades are reported in July; you can call the AP board to receive scores early for a $10 fee.

2. Grades are reported to your home, school, and colleges that you specify with your authorization.

3. If you want to send your scores to additional colleges after you take the exam or want to wait to find out your results before you send them to colleges, you can contact the AP program and have grade reports sent for a fee of $12 per request. All AP scores will be sent to your specified colleges. An additional fee will be charged if you want to withhold scores.

IMPORTANT POINTS TO REMEMBER

1. Regardless of which grade you are in, take the AP exam as soon as you complete the AP course; do not wait until your junior year to do all of your testing.

2. You may attempt to take the AP exam without taking the course.
3. AP tests are similar to college-level exams.
4. AP exams are usually held in May. Check with your guidance counselor for specific AP subject test dates.
5. Keep track of the test registration deadline.
6. Consider buying some guidebooks in that particular subject to help you prepare for the test.
7. Start referring to these guides at least two to three months before the exam date. Work consistently on it for one hour two to three times a week. Increase this frequency as the test dates approaches.
8. By preparing, students are more comfortable walking into the test. The more you know about the subject, the fewer surprises you will have on the test.
9. Check with your teacher for copies of old AP test papers and review these tests.
10. Read all of the directions carefully in advance so you will be familiar with the format and not waste time during your exam.
11. Take practice tests so that you can familiarize yourself with the topics covered.
12. Analyze your strengths and weaknesses and prepare accordingly.
13. Wear comfortable clothes, preferably layers, so that while taking the test if you become too hot or too cold you can adjust accordingly.
14. Have a healthy breakfast the morning of the test. Bring a power snack.
15. When taking the actual tests, read all of the directions thoroughly and all of the questions carefully.
16. Do not get stuck on a question and spend too much time reading that example. Move on to maintain a steady pace.
17. In granting college credit for AP grades, many schools honor scores of 3 or higher. However, the policy for each college differs. Check with the colleges to which you wish to apply.
18. Scoring well on AP exams enhances your application.
19. Send your AP scores to all of the colleges you are applying to.
20. AP scholar recognition is granted to students earning a 3 or better on three AP full-year courses.

FOUR

Tips for Test Taking

[Sheila wrote most of this chapter using her own experience in test taking.]

Whether taking the AP exam or the SAT I or SAT II tests, the following are some general test-taking strategies to help you maximize your test scores. But no matter how prepared you are before test day, there is always an element of nervousness. This is perfectly normal, but keep in mind that this is simply a test. In the case of AP, you can withhold scores. But even if you do not, this is just one test and tests are one factor out of many that colleges look at in determining admission. So keep a positive attitude before and while taking the test, and if you have prepared ahead of time, you are bound to do your best!

TEN USEFUL TIPS FOR BEFORE THE TEST

1. Get plenty of rest on the night before your test date. It is wise to go to bed at a reasonable hour the night before the test.
2. Set your alarm.
3. Eat a healthy breakfast in order to have enough energy to help you make it through your test. Besides, you cannot let any minor distractions such as hunger pangs deter your concentration from your performance.
4. Wear comfortable clothes and dress in layers. By dressing in layers, you can be prepared if the test center is too hot or too cold.
5. Pack a power snack. There will be a short break and you may want to bring a snack such as a power bar, a Milky Way, or a similar food. This snack can give you the sugar-stimulated burst of energy to help you cope through the second half of your exam.
6. Do not cram on the day before the exam. Experience suggests that cramming just will not help and may even make you more anxious. Instead, I found briefly reviewing the test directions, sample ques-

tions, and explanations to be helpful. It may even be helpful to do some sample questions on test day to get you in the mindset.

7. Familiarize yourself with the test format; know the directions ahead of time. Hopefully, by the time you are going to take the test, you will have taken several practice tests. With all of this practice and preparation, you should know and be familiar with the directions for each section of the test. Therefore, on test day you will not have to waste time reading the directions. You can, instead, go straight to the questions. Also, make sure to learn how the tests are scored.

8. Make sure you know the directions to get to the test center and any particular instructions for locating the exact entrance.

9. Set aside plenty of time for setbacks and unforeseen crises, perhaps fifteen minutes more than you think you will need to get to the test center. Try to be there at least thirty minutes before the test. If you do not arrive when the tests begin, you cannot take the test.

10. Have everything that you will need ready the day before the test. Here is a sample checklist:
    - Photo ID with your signature
    - Admission ticket
    - Set of no. 2 pencils
    - Erasers
    - Sharpeners
    - Calculator (with spare batteries or an additional backup calculator)
    - Watch (preferably one that does not beep)

TEN USEFUL TIPS FOR TEST DAY

1. If you feel tense before beginning the test, try to relax; it helps to take a few deep breaths. Remember, being nervous is natural. Experience suggests that a little nervousness can keep your mind sharp and alert. However, too much anxiety can deter you from focusing and performing efficiently.

2. Remember you are in control. Be self-confident and have a positive attitude. These suggestions will allow you to boost up your confidence, concentrate on your test, and do your best.

3. Carefully listen to all of the directions and ask questions if there is anything that you do not comprehend. Carefully read the entire question and do not be in a hurry to answer until you have completely read and understood the question and have weighed each possible answer. This way, you can make sure that you answer the

question asked based on the information provided and not on what you think you already know. Near the end of the tests, questions tend to be harder and trickier to answer. Therefore, it is all the more important to read each question as it comes carefully and thoughtfully so that you do not oversimplify or complicate any question by misreading it.

4. Keep your answer sheet close to your test book to help you mark the correct answer quickly. This also ensures that the correct bubble is marked for the corresponding question.

5. Pace yourself throughout the entire test. At regular intervals, keep track of the time. Try to attempt all of the questions, if possible. Too often students complain that they do not have enough time to complete the tests. But with enough practice, one should be able to find a comfortable pace to go through a test in the specified time limit. Therefore, when test day comes along, you should know not to belabor any one question but to instead answer all the questions you can and then go back to the ones you may have had more trouble with at the end.

6. Concentrate your attention entirely on your work. Do not focus your attention on other test takers who are sneezing, coughing, being fidgety with their pencils, or shaking their legs. Try not to focus on anything except the test in front of you.

7. Remember (in the SAT I) that one section is experimental; it will not count. At the same time, you can never predict which section is experimental so do your best on the entire test.

8. Never rush or get bogged down on any one problem. Usually your first impulse is the best. Do not overthink or overanalyze any of the questions. This will simply waste your time and prevent you from answering more questions that you could get right. At the same time, as you start to answer the harder questions, the obvious answer may not always be the correct one. Keep in mind that you do not have to answer every question in order to do well. Pacing yourself under this undue pressure can stimulate unnecessary paralyzing fear. Experience suggests controlling your adrenaline and being able to concentrate are the key factors of successful test taking.

9. Know when to guess an answer and when to skip a question. If you find a hard question, try not to get stuck. Instead, skip ahead and move on to the next question. Answer the easy questions first. Remember to circle the questions you skipped or to put a big question mark next to the ones where you are unsure about your answers. This way, if you have time at the end you can locate the problem quickly and look back over the debatable answers. Some tests, such as the SAT I, SAT II, and portions of the AP, take points off for

wrong answers. This deduction then leads to the question of whether it is more advantageous to skip a question or to answer it, knowing that you could be wrong. The rule of thumb is that if you can eliminate at least one wrong answer, it is to your advantage to go ahead and answer the question.

10. If you finish your test before your time is up, you may want to use the spare time to reread the questions and verify your answers.

FIVE

Steps in Choosing a College

We can tell you from firsthand experience that choosing a college can be a pretty daunting experience. It is like going through a supermarket and trying to select what to buy without first deciding what you need or how much money you have to spend. Once you know that you need cookies, you can make your search more manageable by limiting yourself to perhaps an aisle. Then you can focus on all of the different kinds of cookies available, such as chocolate, sugar, and cream-filled. You can honestly evaluate your likes and dislikes and limit your selection. Based on your budget, you can target a final range of choices. This process also works with college applications. There are around three thousand U.S. colleges and universities, and if you do not know where to apply, the search can be overwhelming.

To start your search, find out what you are looking for in a college. Evaluate all of the college's features and the admissions criteria. Assess your likes, dislikes, and your academic goals. Then carefully review the specific admissions requirements and match and compare them with your own. It is important to ask yourself if your credentials meet the admissions requirements of a particular college. For example, in a recent interview Sheila asked Dean Fitzsimmons, Harvard dean of admissions: Who is actually admitted based upon the qualifications set forth by the college? He answered:

> An estimated two to three hundred or as many as we can find are the unusually bright, academically oriented individuals. Beyond good grades and SAT scores, these people show a real enthusiasm for learning. A teacher's recommendation letter about them might note that even though the instructor has been teaching for over thirty years and has even taught two Nobel Prize winners, this student is better than all of them. Another two to three hundred students will possess an expertise in one particular area or talent, such as Yo Yo Ma, the famous cellist. The remaining 1,500 or so will be "all-rounders." Most guidebooks say that colleges do not want "all-rounders," but they have long been predominant at Harvard. These people show multiple strengths:

39

outstanding academic and extracurricular accomplishments. We also see outstanding personal qualities in all our students. They often report that one of the most rewarding aspects of their experience at Harvard was the education they received from their fellow classmates. Recommendations from teacher and counselors are extremely helpful to us in identifying the many remarkable individuals who have come here. In fact, many wonderful students are directed our way by high school teachers and counselors who encourage them to apply here.

The whole process is about finding a college that is a perfect match for you, considering your own credentials. For example, you should carefully examine if your SAT scores, along with your class ranking, fall within the range of the middle half of the admitted students scores. If so, then you can view this school as a possible reach school. If your scores put you in the top 25 percent of the admitted students, then you may consider this school as a possible safety school and you may probably want to think about also applying to more selective schools. Finally, if your scores put you in the bottom 25 percent range, then you may regard this school as a dream school and might want to seriously consider also applying to less selective schools to provide a safety net. Although it may seem that the better one's academic qualifications, the better one's odds for admission, that is not always the case. Realize that in applying to a highly selective college such as Harvard, even a perfect SAT score of 1,600 might not guarantee admission. In any case, try to avoid falling into the trap of thinking about admissions only in terms of test scores.

You do not have to rule out your dream school just because you have a mediocre academic profile. With certain credentials, you can enhance your overall profile and improve your chances for admission at highly selective colleges. Unless you fall into a special category of being a minority candidate, then you probably need impressive qualifications such as having an extraordinary dedication to community service or being a nationally recognized athlete to offset favorably your average test scores and/or low class ranking. Since this is one of the most crucial decisions you will make in your life, it is worth investing as much time, energy, and research in it as possible. Then evaluate the list of schools you would like to consider.

How many schools to which to apply is a personal decision, and each applicant, along with his or her parent/guardian and counselors, should individually come to it. Apply to as few as two or as many as ten institutions, for it is your personal choice. Keep in mind, however, that each application takes a lot of your time and money. Remember with Ivy League schools you may not be admitted in spite of having good grades and test scores. Vinay and Sheila felt that applying to several Ivy League schools increased their chances of being accepted by at least one of them.

By junior year, your college search should be in full swing. By the summer after junior year you should be able to compile a list of perhaps ten to fifteen schools as "possibles." To aid your search, create a college journal. Make a list of what you wish to accomplish in college. Focus on the overall quality of the college and on the quality of the particular departments, or academic majors, in which you may be interested. Evaluate and critically compare the features of the various colleges. For serious shoppers, campus visits should help you decide on your final list. Find out the range of test scores of enrolled students instead of admitted students. The range of test scores for admitted students tends to be higher than that of enrolled students because the scores of the top students will be included among the admitted and these students may not actually choose to go to the particular college. Because they are the top students, they may have been using the college as a safety net and may have many colleges from which to choose. Therefore, looking at the range of test scores for enrolled students is a more realistic figure because it is the range for the actual students attending the college.

Set aside some quiet time in order to take a self-evaluation examination by honestly reflecting on your likes and dislikes as well as your strengths and weaknesses. Think about what you want to achieve from attending that particular college. What can you contribute to that institute? Choosing the right college can be an art as well as a science. It takes time, effort, and a readiness to ask yourself some grueling questions about trying to decide to how many colleges to apply, or trying to guess your chances of gaining admission to any particular institution. You must eventually decide with which college to register from those to which you are offered admission. Finally, you must consider what type of college experience you hope to gain in four years and what type of a school is most likely to provide it to you. After analyzing all of these issues, you should be able to modify your list to a manageable number.

As mentioned earlier, choosing a college may seem daunting at first, but if you take things step-by-step you will be just fine. As Woody Allen said, "success is 99 percent hanging on."

Your starting point should be to create a list of the colleges that you would like to explore. Then start gathering data. Do not rely on a single source of information. Fred Hargadon, dean of Princeton admissions, cautions, "Rather than rely on any single source of information, seek out a number of different sources, always keeping in mind the fable aboaut the seven blind philosophers, each of whom, upon touching a different part of an elephant, described the quite different animals they thought it to be. So, too, is the same university likely to be perceived, at least in part, quite differently by its various members" (Hargardon, 2). Therefore, you should explore all the many resources available.

RESOURCES

Print and Internet Sources

1. College guides
    *   *The Peterson's Guide to Four-year Colleges*: a comprehensive guide giving criteria for admissions
    *   *Guide to Colleges*: gives in-depth profiles of over three hundred of the best colleges
    *   The College Board's *The College Handbook*
    *   *ARCO The Right College*: a major directory, noting size, location, and admissions requirements. It also ranks the competitiveness of each college on a six-step scale based on the number of applicants accepted and SAT scores
    *   *Princeton Review Guide to 310 Best Colleges in America*
    *   *Barron's Profiles of American Colleges*
    Some guides give only statistical information while others give both statistical and qualitative information. Check your local library in the reference section for books that provide information about colleges and universities.
2. How-to guides. These offer advice on interviewing, visiting colleges, writing college essays, and filling out the applications. How-to guides such as *A Is for Admission* written by Michele A. Hernández, a Dartmouth admissions officer, are helpful. This book gives you a different perspective of the admissions process because it is written from the point of view of an admissions officer and offers an idea about how the admissions process operates behind closed doors.
3. College catalogs and view books. Look for information on educational opportunities, majors, and courses. A profile of the admitted students' statistical summary information such as test scores can be useful to analyze your chances. As mentioned earlier, the test score range of admitted applicants will be higher than that of the enrolled students.
4. Magazines and newspapers. *Newsweek* and *U.S. News and World Report* publish a special edition on colleges every year. You can get information such as college ranking and a directory of colleges. The *Wall Street Journal*, the *New York Times*, and the *New York Post* have good articles on college admissions from time to time.
5. The Internet. Visit the College Board website at www.collegeboard.org. In addition, many colleges have websites; visit their homepages. Other useful Internet sources provide help with the following:

- Choosing a college. Check out Allaboutcollege.com. This website allows you to search through detailed information on numerous colleges and universities. This complete data site has links to colleges' official websites and offers chat rooms categorized by college, providing prospective students the opportunity to talk with one another.
- Tips on how to apply. Check out www.scholasticregistry.com (Binswanger, 50). If you play an instrument in a band and want to be recruited for it and you have no idea which college band might need you, then turn to this site. It allows you to submit your profile, which in turn will be submitted to several colleges. This way the recruiters can find you if they need you.
- Paying the bills. Click on the paying for college link at http://www.collegeispossible.org/n American Council on Education site. You will find an overview of the different forms of financial aid as well as state-sponsored and institutional aid and information on how to take advantage of educational tax benefits. If you want to be walked through the process of applying for loans, grants, and scholarships, Findaid.org is a good site to visit. The site www.ed.gov/offices/OSFAP/Students has every detail you ever wanted to know about federal student aid programs. At Estudentloan.com you can fill out the on-line loan application and a search engine will match you with up to twelve loan programs-.*Scholarship.com* claims to have a database of more than six hundred thousand college scholarships.
- The ranking game. For ranking, see usnews.com, which does side-by-side comparison (of tuition costs, student-faculty ratio, and the like) of up to four colleges at a time. It also provides the latest ranking of the colleges.

Other Helpful Resources

1. College fairs. Plan to attend these fairs. While there, pick up brochures, talk to admissions personnel, ask questions, and sign up to receive an application or information.
2. Your guidance counselor. Talk to your guidance counselor and find out if he or she has any software with college information. The counselor may also be able to provide you with information about senior students who graduated from a particular college or who are currently attending the school.
3. College visits. After your campus visit, focus on a realistic target of schools to apply to. (See chapter 6 on college visits for details.)
4. People related to the school. Talk to someone who is currently attending or has attended that college. Meet alumni, friends, relatives, and senior students.

COMPARING AND EVALUATING
COLLEGE FEATURES

Diversity

1. Look at all the issues such as gender, race, economic factors, geographical mix, and social background.
2. Find out who comprises the student body mix.
3. How diverse is the student body population?
4. What are your preferences?

Cost

1. Are you considering an Ivy League school, in-state college, out-of-state college, or a private college?
2. All of these differences can determine the cost of tuition. For example, in-state fees are far less than out-of-state costs. In addition, some in-state schools award full scholarships based on academic merit.
3. Different schools offer different financial programs to students.
4. Check the criteria for scholarship eligibility.
5. Factor in all other costs such as books and room and board.

Academic Features

1. What is the quality of the faculty and their credentials?
2. Look into how many professors have doctorates.
3. Are there any research opportunities for students?
4. How difficult is it to get a research job?
5. Are there any study abroad programs?
6. Do graduate students or professors teach the courses?
7. Are there any academic counseling services to meet the special needs of freshmen?
8. What educational opportunities and majors are offered?
9. Is the curriculum rigorous enough for you, or is it too rigorous? Will you be challenged?
10. Is the testing intense or easy?
11. Are there lots of majors from which to choose?
12. Find out if the colleges will award you AP credits.
13. What are the specific graduation requirements?
14. Find out about the available honors program.
15. How easy is it for students to get all of the classes for which they sign up?

16. Look into all of these features carefully and determine which factors are important for you.

Selectivity

1. What is the number of applicants that the college has received in the last few years?
2. How many students are admitted each year (admit ratio)?
3. What is the range of test scores of the admitted students?
4. Does your academic record fall within the admissions criteria?
5. Check out the retention rate (what percentage of the first year students return or transfer the next year).

School Size

Find out the student population of the school. It is easy to stand out in small schools. Do you want to be a big fish in a small pond or a small fish in a big pond? In small schools, classes are usually taught by professors who are easily accessible to students. On the other hand, large schools offer a lot of educational opportunities. There are usually more majors and classes from which to choose and more professors to choose from. Approximate definitions of school size are as follows:

1. Small schools (fewer than 2,000 students)
2. Medium schools (2,000–5,000 students)
3. Large schools (5,000–10,000 students)
4. Very large schools (over 10,000 students)

Class Size

1. Do you prefer to learn in large lecture halls?
2. Are you comfortable taking a course with over three hundred students?
3. Do you prefer a small class size?
4. Are you comfortable in a course with fewer than twenty students?
5. Look at the student-faculty ratio.
6. Find out if it is easy to interact with the professors.

Climate

1. Is the weather too hot for you?
2. Is the weather too cold for you?

3. Is the weather pleasant?
4. What are your preferences?

Campus/Student Life

1. What is the quality of the student life? Are the students friendly or competitive?
2. How many hours do students study?
3. What are the weekend activities for the students?
4. How is the social life?
5. How safe is the campus? Get a copy of the college campus security report, which will provide you with information on the college security policies and campus crime statistics.
6. Is the campus located in a suburban setting, like Duke University, a rural setting, like Dartmouth College, or in the middle of a city, like George Washington University?
7. A big city has a lot of cultural activities to offer.
8. The crime rate is a major concern in a city.
9. Check out the cafeteria food.
10. Visit the campus to answer most of these questions.

Dorms

1. Are the dorms available to all of the freshman students?
2. Are they co-ed or single sex? What are your preferences?
3. Are there fraternities/sororities to consider?
4. Do you have to make your own accommodations?

Location

1. What is the distance from home?
2. There are advantages and disadvantages to both options.
3. If you move too far, you cannot visit home frequently.
4. If you stay close, you could bring your laundry home.
5. Would you prefer to be within two hours driving distance?
6. Do you mind staying far away from home and flying to commute?
7. Look at alternate means of public transportation for the commute.
8. Can you keep a car?
9. Is it economical for you to commute by plane?

Sports

1. Do you want to play for their varsity team?
2. Does the college offer intramural or club-level recreational sports?

3. How are the athletic facilities?
4. What are your chances of participating in intercollegiate and/or intramural sports?

ASSESSING OTHER MEASUREMENTS

Admissions Criteria

1. What are the test score requirements? What GPA is necessary, and what grades are considered adequate by the institution?
2. How do your credentials match up with these requirements?
3. Further refine your list of colleges to which to apply.

Statistical Ratios

Another measure to which we paid close attention was the matriculation rate. By definition, this is the percentage of admitted applicants who opt to enroll. A matriculation rate of 50 percent or more accepted students enrolled in the college indicates that many applicants considered the school as their top choice of college. A yield of less than 25 percent indicates that the applicant used this college as a safety school. Carefully examine all the following ratios:

1. Admit rate: the number of applications received compared to how many students are accepted
2. Yield ratio: the number of students accepted compared to how many enrolled
3. Retention rate: what percentage of students return for their sophomore year?

Academic Index (AI) Formula

As Michele A. Hernández notes in her *A Is for Admission*, many Ivy League schools use a rating system known as the academic index (AI) for assessing the individual applicant's qualifications. The AI is a precise mathematical formula derived by summing three factors: (1) the average of your highest SAT I verbal section and math section test scores; (2) the average of your highest three SAT II subject test scores; and (3) your GPA (capped at 4.0) times 20 *or* your converted rank score (CRS). (CRS is derived from your class ranking and a conversion table.) Each section's test scores are rounded to two places. For example, 800 will be 80, giving you a total score ranging between 0 and 240. These values are further broken down to rank students on a scale. For example, at Dartmouth, AI is based on a scale of 1 to 9, with 9 being the highest. An applicant with an academic index of 8 or 9 has a very good chance of being accepted to almost any college he or she applies to. On the other hand, Harvard uses a scale of 1 to 6, with 1 being the highest. (For detailed information on the academic index, see Hernández, chapter 6.) To some extent this can give you an understanding of how the admissions officers rank your application and gauge your chances for admission. This way, you can take the necessary steps to improve your profile.

Choosing a Major

Choosing a major can be important at a highly competitive college. For example, my son applied with an interest in becoming a biology major (pre-med), which is a popular major. In certain schools, acceptance rates in popular majors may be lower than in nontraditional majors. For example, computer science at MIT is a competitive major. Though the temptation exists, applicants should not use misleading majors to get in, as admissions officers can determine your interest by looking at your extracurricular activities, essay topics, and discussions from your interview. If you are not sure of a major, you can choose "undecided." My daughter was not sure if she was interested in law or business, so she applied as "undecided." As a freshman in college, she wanted to explore new subjects with an open mind and take advantage of the full range of educational opportunities and programs that the colleges had to offer.

MODIFYING YOUR LIST

By this point you should be able to modify your list of target schools by selecting college features that are important to you. Most students apply to anywhere from six to eight colleges, but again, this is a personal choice.

A rule of thumb to follow is to make sure that you apply to at least two colleges within each degree of selectivity (safe choice colleges, good choice colleges, and top choice colleges), giving a total of at least six schools on your list.

1. Safe choice colleges: where chances of admissions are more than 50 percent
2. Good choice colleges: where chances of admissions are 50/50
3. Top choice colleges: where chances of admissions are less than 50 percent

Keep in mind, colleges need you, too. Good candidates are their most valuable assets. Good luck with your search!!

Six

College Visits

How many of us actually believe the college visit to be a key factor in our determination of college choice? Just how important is your college visit? As noted in the *Official Visitors Guide to Boston and Its Top Colleges*: "71% of students surveyed in a recent *Money Magazine* poll said campus visits were the most useful strategy in helping them choose a college."

When my son was in high school, we did not place much importance on college visits. When he was in tenth grade, he went to a summer program in Boston where they had arranged several campus tours for colleges in that area. Not knowing any better, we did not think to revisit these colleges when he decided to apply to them because he had already seen them once before. Little did we know that the campus visit plays a crucial role in the college admission and application process. We did not realize how premature campus visits in tenth grade are, especially if they were his only visits. At that age, students are not serious shoppers and do not know what to look for in a college or how to compare the strengths of college departments to one another. In addition, many students at that age are not definite about college majors or, needless to say, their future career plans. The fact of the matter is that at such an early age, the concept of even going to college has not been set in the minds of students who have only completed their second year of high school. Now we have learned to casually and not critically consider the early visits made before tenth grade. There is a big difference in maturity level when comparing a tenth grade student to one who has completed eleventh grade. In the summer after the junior year, a young individual is lot more serious about college admission and hence starts to pay close attention to all of the college facilities and admission criteria.

College visits can also uncover a lot of useful information, such as the strength of its various academic departments. By eleventh grade students have some inclination as to what direction of study they are considering. These visits can clarify their thinking, helping them make sound choices as to which major to pursue.

WHY A CAMPUS VISIT?

Without a doubt, a campus visit can be an excellent time to assist students in making up their minds on possible college choices. These applications take a lot of time, and a common problem that students make is applying to too many colleges. Applying to too many schools will create an extra burden on the child and unnecessarily dilute the student's effort. This often compromises the student's quality of the application for quantity of content. This search stimulated my daughter to think twice about certain colleges and determine whether she even wanted to apply to them at all. Ultimately she was able to update and modify the number of schools to apply to and eliminate three colleges from her list. By concentrating on fewer applications, she was able to give her best possible effort in completing them. This extra time allowed her to write and rewrite her essays leisurely and meticulously.

Along with being an excellent planning tool, campus visits are a key element in the early admission decision. Based on their initial impression, applicants may even change their minds as to which college to apply to for early decision. For example, my daughter wanted to apply to a certain highly selective college for early admission. After the campus visit, she had second thoughts about applying to that particular college for early admission. She had some hesitation about the town and was not ready to commit to the school, whose early admission was binding. She needed more time to think this through and decided to apply to Harvard, MIT, and Georgetown for early action because their decision was not binding. She could still apply to that college for regular decision and keep her options open.

Campus visits made the application process real for my daughter and motivated her to set higher goals for which to strive in order to meet the standards of the admission requirements of a particular college that she really liked. Campus visits can also help students project themselves as prospective candidates, which stimulates them not only to set higher goals but also to work consistently harder to make these goals attainable. This result is the reward of finally getting admitted to that college.

ADVICE FOR APPROACHING THE COLLEGE VISIT

Preparation

To make the visit as informative as possible, gather as much information and learn all about these colleges *before* your visit. Make notes about each school. Just before each visit, refer to your notes and refresh your memory about that college. This was particularly helpful for my children when we visited more than one university per day or per trip. This way, if you have any questions or concerns you will remember to address them first during your visit.

Before you leave home, make sure to get maps and travel directions. Make hotel reservations for the overnight stays. Read college brochures and look at the campus maps before the visit. You can save a lot of time by deciding where to go for information on campus, and you will know exactly what activities are recommended for visitors. Call ahead and get instructions for visitors' parking. Call and check to make sure that your visits do not conflict with any college activities, such as exam week, parents' weekend, or a big college game, since the college will be very crowded and may not be appropriate to visit.

Scheduling

When convenient, it is helpful to schedule two separate campus visits for a particular school that is on the candidate's top priority list. Plan your first visit during the summer vacation after junior year when the pressures of schoolwork do not burden the student. Besides, at that time colleges are not very crowded. Call ahead to check schedules on tours and information sessions. If required, make reservations for these activities. It is always wise to arrive at least fifteen minutes before a tour or information session. This way you will have enough time to get familiar with the campus and find your way. Start the day by taking a tour. Current students conduct most tours; use this opportunity to ask them questions. Later you may want to attend an information session conducted by admissions staff for general college information. At the end of most sessions, listeners get an opportunity to ask questions. Examples of questions include: Does Harvard allow applicants to apply to more than one college early action who have similar early action programs? How many of your freshmen courses are taught by graduate students instead of university professors? How is the faculty advising system arranged in this university? Such questions are appropriate. Check the length of each activity and make sure that the campus tour does not overlap with the information session that you plan to attend.

In our experience, it was easier to schedule appointments in June compared to slots in late July and August. The tours and information sessions were always more crowded with visitors in the second half of the summer. However, the advantage of making a trip in late August is that some colleges are in session and visitors can see the normal campus activity and have more opportunities to talk with current students. (Spring break of your junior year is another option.) This choice is extremely useful if you are planning only one trip to that campus. Whatever your strategy, plan your visits accordingly and inform the colleges well in advance. Planning is the key to make the most of your visits.

Consider the fall of the senior year to make your second visit and explore alone this time. This way you can see the campus in action. All campus visits are informative and exciting; however, if you visit when the classes are in session, it is more valuable. Students should plan to spend a night on campus, if convenient. If you know someone on campus, you may consider spending a night with him or her. If not, call the college and find out if they make any such arrangements. With this arrangement you can spend time in the bookstore, attend a class, look at the bulletin boards along the hallway, talk to the students, visit a social event, talk to some admissions personnel, and try to get a feel of what staying at that particular college will be like. Get the e-mail addresses of students you meet so that you can ask questions that you may think of after your visit. Some colleges sponsored overnight programs for my children and encouraged them to participate once they were admitted and considered prospective candidates.

Helpful Hints

To organize your series of visits, try to coordinate all of the college visits from the same geographic area in one trip. We planned our visit to Dartmouth, MIT, and Harvard all in the same trip. However, make sure you spend at least three or four hours on each campus. Try to limit to one college per day and at the most, two. Try not to do too many on the same visit, for you will be overwhelmed and confused with all of the information. If you are serious about a certain college and it is one of your top priority schools, you should plan to spend at least half of a day. Eat at the local restaurants, visit the tourist information center, and get a feel for the college and the community around it.

Think Interviews

While planning college visits, set up a campus interview, if convenient. Check with each college regarding the deadline for college interviews. In our experience most colleges conducted college interviews through December. The interview appointment slots get filled up fast, so call early!

Think carefully about the trip that lies ahead of you. Road trips, especially the long-distance ones, can be very exhausting. We tried to schedule the campus interview on either a Monday or Friday, for this way we could combine it with the weekend and spend time leisurely looking around the campus, hence not blurring our impression of the school. We completed most of the campus interviews in the summer along with our campus visits. This way, if we had to take an extra day for travel it would not conflict with our children's schoolwork, sports activities, and personal time. Students are more relaxed in the summer and have plenty of time to read all of the information about the college. With this preparation they can come across to the interviewer as being ready for the interview. Being prepared is particularly important because this gives the child the self-assurance and confidence that he or she needs before the interview. Nothing can be more fatal than a child arriving unprepared to a campus interview with his or her mind preoccupied about other things such as an important sports competition, a missed school dance, or a makeup test.

Food for Thought

Finally, when visiting a campus, create a journal. Did you gain any useful information from this visit? Were you impressed with any particular features of the college? What are your observations about the college? Sit down and take time to record all of your thoughts in your journal while the experience is still fresh in your mind. For every college that you visit, write down the pros, cons, and your comments and evaluations. (See the sample chart at the end of this chapter.) This information will be useful later when objectively comparing all the options of perspective colleges and will be one of the critical elements in narrowing your tentative list of colleges.

To add to your notes, write down the name and address of the admissions personnel who interviewed you. Make sure to record your visit by filling out visiting sheets available at the admissions office. In today's competitive environment, your visit not only reflects your interest in that college but also enhances the application because admissions officers will notice a student who is seriously considering their school. In addition, these forms also ensure that you will be on their mailing list to receive an application.

As a final note, if you are missing high school classes, stop by the admissions office and get a written confirmation of your visit to submit to your school. At our high school, students were allowed a certain number of excused absent days for college visits. If you need to take an excused absence for a college visit, choose the day wisely, attempting not to miss scheduled tests and exams. Lastly, you may want to meet with financial admission officers.

IMPORTANT POINTS TO REMEMBER
BEFORE A CAMPUS VISIT

1. Make a list of colleges that you would like to explore. (See chapter 5 on choosing a college for details.)
2. Gather as much information as possible from various sources such as college view books, college guides, handbooks, brochures, and the Internet.
3. Thoroughly read all of the publications about these colleges. Familiarize yourself with all of the features/facilities that these colleges have, such as size, levels of diversity, and academic programs.
4. Ask yourself what your personal goals and career objectives are. Do the colleges' features suit your needs? Do they have the educational opportunities for you? Do the schools meet your preferences, such as living in a city versus a college town?
5. Evaluate these colleges based on admissions criteria requirements.
6. Does your high school preparation match these college admission recommendations?
7. Refine some of your answers and establish a wide range of colleges that match your preferences.
8. Consider visiting some of these colleges.
9. Consider having your first visits during the summer between the junior and senior year.
10. Plan two campus visits for each college you are seriously considering.
11. Plan in order to make the most of your college campus visits. Make notes about each college. Just before each visit, refresh your memory by referring to your notes about that particular college. Then if you have any questions or concerns you can answer these inquiries during your visit.
12. Call the colleges at least three weeks prior to your visit and make appointments for interviews, if appropriate.
13. Also call ahead and check schedules on tours and information sessions, making reservations as needed.
14. Note all the times of the tours and information sessions, keeping track of the length of any activity you plan to attend.
15. Plan to spend at least three or four hours per campus.
16. Coordinate all of the campus visits from the same geographic area in one trip.
17. Obtain all of the necessary road maps and travel directions.
18. Call ahead and get the visitors' parking information at the campus.
19. Make hotel reservations, if appropriate.
20. Consider making a second visit alone in the fall of your senior year

when the campus is in action and stay overnight at the college, if convenient. (Junior year during your high school's spring break is another possible option to see the campus in action.)

21. Make sure to get the e-mail addresses of several students that you talk to so that you can ask any questions that you may have after your visit.
22. Remember to stop at the admissions office and fill out a visitor's form. Make sure you are on their mailing list to receive an application.
23. Create a college visit notebook during your visit. For every college that you visit, write down the pros and cons that you would like to remember. This information is useful when comparing colleges.
24. If you are missing high school, stop at the admissions office to get a written confirmation of your visit.
25. By this point you should be able to zero in on some of the colleges to which you would like to apply.
26. Along with being an excellent planning tool, campus visits are a key element in the early admission decision.

SHEILA'S OBSERVATIONS ON DARTMOUTH COLLEGE

1. Educational Opportunities

Rating: (on scale of 1-10)   1   2   3   4   5   6   <u>7</u>   8   9   10
Pros: **Seeks to provide students with a broad-based education; requires incoming students to take a freshman seminar and composition course.**
Cons: **College is in session year round, offering four ten-week terms per year. Required to stay on campus summer after sophomore year.**
Your comments: **Some students like the year-round program because it allows them to schedule their own agendas and leaves room to allow students to study abroad.**

2. Academic Qualities (research opportunities, student-faculty ratio)

Rating: (on scale of 1–10)   1   2   3   4   5   6   7   8   <u>9</u>   10
Pros: **Professors are very accessible.**
Cons:
Your comments: **Professors and students seem to have a close relationship. Students are often invited to professors' houses for dinner, even on holidays like Thanksgiving. Students even baby-sit for professors.**

3. Campus Safety and Diversity

Rating: (on scale of 1–10)   1   2   3   4   5   6   7   8   <u>9</u>   10
Pros: **One of the safest campuses in U.S.**
Cons:
Your comments: **Does not seem very diverse (5 rating for diversity).**

4. Location, Size, and Weather Conditions
Rating: (on scale of 1–10)   1   2   3   4   <u>5</u>   6   7   8   9   10
Pros: **Medium-sized campus.**
Cons: **Rural, two hours from closest big city (Boston).**
Your comments: **Weather may be harsh especially for walking around, going to and from classes.**

5. Student Life, Housing, and Social Activities

Rating: (on scale of 1–10)   1   2   3   4   5   <u>6</u>   7   8   9   10
Pros: **Greek system (With frat row) exists but does not dominate. Big on traditions, for example, winter carnival where they have snow sculptors, ice-skating, skiing, etc.**

Cons: **Most of the social life is only based on campus because there is no town/city.**
Your comments:

6. General Observation:
Picturesque campus. Students are friendly.

SAMPLE SURVEY FORM

1. Educational Opportunities
Rating: (on scale of 1–10)　　1　　2　　3　　4　　5　　6　　7　　8　　9　　10
Pros:
Cons:
Your comments:

2. Academic Qualities (research opportunities, student-faculty ratio)
Rating: (on scale of 1–10)　　1　　2　　3　　4　　5　　6　　7　　8　　9　　10
Pros:
Cons:
Your comments:

3. Campus Safety and Diversity
Rating: (on scale of 1–10)　　1　　2　　3　　4　　5　　6　　7　　8　　9　　10
Pros:
Cons:
Your comments:

4. Location, Size, and Weather Conditions
Rating: (on scale of 1–10)　　1　　2　　3　　4　　5　　6　　7　　8　　9　　10
Pros:
Cons:
Your comments:

5. Student Life, Housing, and Social Activities
Rating: (on scale of 1–10)　　1　　2　　3　　4　　5　　6　　7　　8　　9　　10
Pros:
Cons:
Your comments:

6. General Observation

SEVEN

The Interview

PREPARING FOR YOUR COLLEGE INTERVIEW

[Sheila wrote this from personal experience.]

No matter whether your interview is with an admissions officer on a college campus or with a local alumnus, your preparation for the interview is the same. There are a few tips and tricks that you can follow for a successful interview, but the most important skill to perfect is maintaining your confidence while still being polite and respectful. Do not act overconfident, but at the same time do not act too timid. Try to maintain eye contact during the interview. The key is to *be yourself*. Do not try to act like someone you are not. Be self-assured in the questions you ask in the interview and in the responses to those asked of you. One single interview cannot terribly hurt your chances for acceptance. On the other hand, if you have a great interview with a key admissions officer, it is bound to help!

Before your interview, take a self-analysis test. Ask yourself broad-based yet probing questions. For example, consider why you are interested in college X? What can you contribute to that college? What are your strengths and weaknesses? When thinking about questions that you may be asked, consider the following experiences. I had interviews (both on campus and with alumni) with practically all of the eight colleges to which I applied. In my experience, the opening question that nearly every interviewer (especially admissions officers) asked was to tell them about myself. Now this can be a very intimidating and daunting question, but if it is broken into smaller sections, it is a great opportunity for you to take control of the interview. The essential purpose behind the interview is for the interviewer to see how well you can communicate. At the same time, they genuinely want to learn a little more about you as a person. Tell them about yourself. I would tackle this question by dividing it into three areas:

59

1. Academic experience
2. Extracurricular experience
3. Personal, religious, and community experience

Admissions officers and alumni have to do a write-up about the interview, usually in categories similar to these. Know ahead of time what you will say in each area, and that should prepare you for most of your interview. Do not be too prerehearsed or sound programmed. Your interview, like a conversation, should be very natural. Ultimately, whatever you talk about you should talk about it in depth, with enthusiasm and with passion. Remember to thank the interviewer for his or her time at the conclusion of the interview and to ask for a business card in order to get the interviewer's full name, title, and the address. After the interview, promptly write and mail a thank-you note.

HELPFUL TIPS

1. Read the college booklets and brochures and learn all about the college before your interview. Before a campus interview, take a tour or attend an information session in order to get added information. Being prepared and familiar with the college is crucial because this gives you the confidence that you need before the interview and proves that you are genuinely interested in the institution.
2. Locate the place of the interview ahead of time. This allows you to relax and be yourself instead of fretting to find the place in the few minutes before the interview.
3. Be punctual; preferably, come a few minutes earlier than your appointment time.
4. What should you wear for the interview? You may call ahead and ask what is the dress code for the interview. If not, consider dresses, skirts, and dress pants for women, and ties, dress shirts, and blazers (optional) for men.
5. There is no single set of good answers that applies to your interview questions. But be honest with your answers.
6. Do not mention your SAT scores unless specifically asked about them.
7. Be alert at all times of your interview. Remember admissions officers are always looking for signs of motivation and initiative in applicants.
8. You may bring a résumé or any artwork material that you would like to share with the interviewer. For example, I had hand painted switch plates and sold them to raise money to purchase peanut but-

ter and jelly sandwiches for a homeless shelter. I took samples of my switch plates to share with the interviewer. I also carried the brochure and article on the Community Foundation project that I was involved in. Although it is not required to bring these supplementary materials, it can provide an additional insight into your unique talents and personality.

9. Use the interview as an opportunity to get valuable information, both academic and nonacademic, about the college and to increase your chances of admission.

10. Colleges are dynamic organizations with their ever-changing admissions policies, such as early admissions/early action programs. While most quantitative facts, such as cost, class size, and admit rate are relatively easy to come by, other qualitative information, such as how much do students get to interact with their professors, is not as easily found. Think about what it is that you would want to know about the college. Bring a list of questions that you would like to ask the interviewer, but a rule of thumb is, do *not* ask questions that can easily be found and answered in the college's literature.

11. Save the best for last. Keep the interview of your top choice colleges last, so that you will have some experience and have built some confidence from the previously conducted interviews.

12. Get a business card from your interviewer, or full name and title, so that you can promptly send a thank-you note.

TYPES OF INTERVIEWS

On-Campus Interviews

Interviews on campus are usually conducted with an admissions officer or admissions personnel. In our experience, some colleges, such as Yale and Dartmouth, allow students to conduct on-campus interviews. Depending on the college, campus interviews are more broad-based and general and usually short (thirty minutes).

Alumni Interviews

Alumni interviews conducted locally are, in my experience, a little more challenging than those on campus. Alumni usually ask many specific questions. When I had one alumni interview with an alumna of a prestigious college, she asked me questions that were sent from the college. I assume this is standard procedure for alumni interviews, and this is why they ask more specific questions. They may even ask about current events. Stay relaxed and do not think too much about your answers. A more natural response to a question is better than one with perfect content or one that is too prerehearsed.

QUESTIONS YOU MAY BE ASKED

These are some that were asked at the interviews.

1. What has been your greatest accomplishment so far?
2. What books have you read recently? What was your favorite book? Why?
3. What did you do this summer?
4. What do you hope to gain by attending this college?
5. How can you contribute to the school?
6. If you had the opportunity to do something differently in your high school years, what would that be?
7. What major are you planning to pursue?
8. What is your favorite pastime? Hobbies?
9. Tell me something about your family.
10. What are your strongest and weakest points?
11. What have you done to prepare for college?
12. What was your greatest experience in high school?
13. Tell me about your interests.
14. Tell me about your involvement in extracurricular activities.
15. What accomplishments are you most proud of?
16. Which teacher has had a significant impact on your life?
17. How would you spend a day off from school?
18. How would someone who knows you well describe you?

QUESTIONS YOU MAY ASK

Try to think of at least three questions to ask at the end of your interview. These can be as easy to come up with as asking about something in which you are interested. For example, if you are interested in debate, you can ask whether the college has a debate team or what that college's status is in that particular area.

When asking questions, *do not* ask commonly asked questions (that is, questions found in the handbook of the college, especially with an on-campus interview). For example, do not ask any statistical information such as class size if that information is already mentioned in the handbook. Instead, read all your college brochures before the interview.

Here are some possible questions.

1. Are there any research projects with the professors, and how difficult is it to get one as a freshman?
2. How is the student advising service organized? When are students assigned an advisor, and does he or she counsel them about course selection in their freshman year?
3. You may inquire (at a university) if graduate students teach and grade papers for the undergraduate class.
4. Ask questions and voice concerns about freshman housing, such as how many students share a room.
5. How easy or difficult is it to get the classes that the students sign up for in their freshman year?
6. Are there any special programs customized to specifically address a freshman's needs?
7. How much do the students get to interact with the professors?
8. What is the level of academic difficulty as a freshman, and what support programs are designed to counsel the freshman to help him or her cope? (Since students come from different types of schools, each has a different level of knowledge and comprehension of a subject, and some may need additional outside help while others may be very prepared for a course.)
9. Ask about the following in terms of the specific college:
   - Admit rate: the number of applications they receive compared to how many students are accepted
   - Yield ratio: the number of students accepted compared to how many are enrolled
   - Retention rate: the percentage of students who return for their sophomore year.

THE PARENTS' ROLE

As parents, we felt it was very important to maintain a calm, self-assured, and positive attitude before the interview. It was vital not to display any emotions such as anxiety or nervousness, all of which are understandable. Your kids are already going through all of these emotions, and it would not help them for you, as a parent, to compound their fears by getting anxious as well. Your kids are looking for your moral support.

Remember that it is natural for your kids to experience these jitters before the interview. Trust me to just hang in there. It will be just fine. I found it helpful to give them positive reinforcement. Sometimes my kids needed a pat to get motivated; other times they needed encouragement to boost their self-esteem. As observed, some kids just needed assurance to avoid paralyzing fear. Talk to your kids (that is, if they are up to it) on lighter topics such as where they want to go to eat or to sightsee later. I learned to *never* give them any last-minute advice or to have a disagreement or a power struggle with them (regardless of who is right) before the interview. We would remember to stay calm and to maintain a positive attitude.

My kids could sense our attitudes, and it reflected on how confident they felt. It also gave them the reassurance that they needed before an interview. Trust me, kids always appreciate your support, though they may not always express it. My kids always told me how much they appreciated our help and support later—but much later.

We also found it was helpful to drop our daughter at the interview place and leave her alone a few minutes before the interview, for more than one reason. It gave her the time and space to be calm and collected before the interview. It also reflected her confidence and independence We would use that time to walk around the campus, but we always made sure to return before the interview was over. In our campus interview experience in almost all of the colleges, the interviewer always looked forward to meeting us, the parents, and wanted to know if we had any questions.

As parents, we felt it was important to let our daughter handle any questions relating to college admissions, since she was the one seeking admission. This also displays maturity on the student's part. Instead, as parents, we often asked questions about campus safety, the quality of cafeteria food, or freshman housing. We also addressed our specific concerns. For example, our daughter was in cross-country and loved to run, and we wanted to know how safe was it for students to jog around the campus.

General questions parents usually ask are:

1. Is the food any good?
2. Is the campus safe?
3. How often do students go home on weekends?
4. [Asked of students] What do you like the most or the least about this college?
5. [Asked of students] Why did you choose this college?

As parents we always dressed comfortably yet neat and presentable. Most of the colleges we visited were located far from where we lived. So we would try to arrive a night before, if time permitted. We found this beneficial first because the extra time gave us the opportunity to walk around the campus and familiarize our kids with the college, the place of the interview, and the neighborhood. Moreover, the kids could relax and not be too tired from the traveling before the interview.

We scheduled the interviews during the summer break before the senior year. This way our children did not have the added pressure of making up schoolwork or tests or missing their extracurricular activities. We would call ahead (at least three weeks) and set up the appointment. We would also inquire about campus tour hours and information session timings. We would find out if appointments were needed for the like, and we would try to fit these activities around the interview timing. We found it was advantageous for the students to attend the information session before the interview. With this preparation they would gain added knowledge about the college and come across as well prepared for the interview.

Make sure you sign in at the admissions office and fill out a visitation sheet during your college visits. This step allows you to be on their mailing list for a college application.

MOCK INTERVIEW: THE "FOURS" EXERCISES

Many students are nervous about the interview process, but you can help them by conducting this simple exercise. Ask them the following questions and any others that come to mind. This can help ease their tension about being intimidated or caught off-guard by any question that might be asked at the interview. This activity can also be helpful in making students feel comfortable and confident before the interview. In order to make the interview process less intimidating, you can practice this exercise with your child to familiarize and prepare him or her before the actual interview.

1. Help them to create four questions to ask the interviewer.
2. Choose four of their unique strengths that they would like to emphasize and that would let the interviewer know about them, thus enhancing their chances of admission.
3. List four reasons why they are interested in applying to this college.
4. Create four commonly asked questions, and quiz them on the list.

IMPORTANT POINTS TO REMEMBER

1. Be prepared. Read all of the booklets and brochures about the college before your interview.

2. Review some of the commonly asked questions.
3. Be punctual, preferably a few minutes earlier than your appointment time.
4. Either an admissions officer or admissions personnel conducts campus interviews in most highly selective colleges. In some colleges, such as Yale and Dartmouth, the students conduct the on-campus interview.
5. Local alumni in your area conduct alumni interviews.
6. In our experience, most highly selective colleges conduct both alumni and on-campus interviews.
7. What should you wear for the interview? You may call ahead and ask what is the dress code for the interview. Dress appropriately, not slick.
8. Be honest with your answers.
9. Be yourself at the interview.
10. Do not mention your SAT scores unless specifically asked about them.
11. Be alert at all times during your interview.
12. You may bring a résumé or any artwork material that you would like to share with the interviewer. Although it is not required to bring these supplementary materials, it can provide additional insight into your unique talents and personality.
13. Think of some carefully thought out questions that you would like to ask the interviewer.
14. Do not ask any questions that are already mentioned in the college brochures and handbooks.
15. Use the interview as an opportunity to get valuable information about the college and increase your chances of admission.
16. Promptly send thank-you notes to your interviewer.
17. Save the best for last. Schedule the interview for your top choice colleges last, and this way you will have some experience and build some confidence from the previous interviews.

EIGHT

The Application

Going through the college application process can be one of the most exciting and rewarding experiences for both students and their parents/guardians, yet it can also be a frequently overwhelming, often bewildering, and extremely stressful time. Most application forms are mailed in late summer or early fall of the senior year. It is usually during this time of year that students are taking the most challenging courses and also attempting their standardized tests. In addition, many high school seniors rise to leadership positions in their extracurricular activities and in varsity sports. All of these demands can easily dilute the student's efforts when completing his or her application. Thus, parents and guardians must play an active role in assisting the students whenever needed.

College office hours are usually 9 A.M. to 5 P.M. Since most students are busy either with schoolwork or with after-school activities, it is quite understandable to have parents or guardians call colleges on their children's behalf for various reasons such as setting up a campus interview, requesting an application, or confirming that an application is complete. In addition, parents may help students in the following ways:

1. Making sure all of the college applications are received
2. Keeping track of approaching application deadlines
3. Typing of applications as needed
4. Following up with the recommendation letter reminders. Students have to struggle between classes to find their guidance counselors and teachers to give them the recommendation letters and then hastily leave for after-school activities. Thus, it becomes increasingly difficult for students to keep track and follow up on these recommendation letters. Parents can get involved by requesting that the guidance counselor collect all of the teachers' recommendation letters and mail the completed application along with their guidance evaluation form and application fees on time

67

5. Requesting that the Educational Testing Service report the test scores to all prospective colleges
6. Making sure that all the AP test scores are mailed to the appropriate colleges
7. Following up on any additional transcripts to be mailed to colleges from courses taken during summer school or college credits earned while their child is still in high school
8. Keeping a file with all of the college application parts
9. Making copies of completed applications to use as a backup. (Also, request that the guidance counselor make a copy of his/her evaluation)
10. Mailing all of the college applications

Although parents can assist students in many ways during the application process, the bulk of the responsibility rests with the students. The best strategy is planning; start early and well before the applications are out. If you are disciplined enough to organize parts of your application, such as ranking the list of activities and writing generic essays based on frequently asked topics in the summer before your senior year, then you will be ahead of the game. If, however, you are the type of applicant who will never be motivated to plan ahead, a disciplined approach of one hour set aside for a couple of days a week can help you accomplish a lot. When it comes time for application deadlines, you will be glad you stayed on track. Also, this strategic planning allows you to focus on other details such as sending test scores to the prospective colleges and promptly mailing all the parts of the applications, all of which can substantially improve your chances for admission.

Another reason it is important to start early is so that you can send in your applications early. Common sense suggests that admissions officers may be more inclined to be generous with the admissions in the beginning of the search when there are still more places available. They may become very selective as these vacancies get filled up and when the admissions office is flooded with stacks of applications. As the deadline approaches and there are volumes of applications to be processed, officers are forced to be very selective when evaluating and admitting applicants competing for the same limited spots, just as on Halloween, when at the start you have a lot of candy and are very generous when handing it out. Admissions personnel carefully examine what is presented to them in each application at this time. However, as your candy stock gets low and you still have several groups of kids knocking on your door with over half an hour to go, you may become stingier in handing out the candy. So, too, admissions officers may become tightfisted in granting admissions when there are few spots left and many applications yet to be processed. Early in the evening on Halloween you are easily impressed by any creative costume, but after a while, when you have seen several good costumes, you are not as easily impressed. Admissions officers also appreciate each individual more before they have seen the same profile repeatedly. In the beginning of the reading process, officers may be easily impressed with a good essay, but later when they have already read several exceptional essays, even an outstanding essay may not so easily make an impact on them. Also, in the beginning, they may have a lot of time to leisurely read all of the application details. When faced with a volume of applicants, officers may only take an overview.

Also, when considering your application strategy, mailing your application early is particularly crucial for rolling admissions where applications are read and processed as they arrive. Another strong incentive for starting the application process early is that you have the luxury of going over the application and making any corrections as needed without having to anguish about the approaching deadline. Sheila started processing all of her college applications very early, especially the ones on her top choice list. Once she had completed her application, she would walk away from it for a few days and come back to proofread it with a fresh vision and an objective approach.

Think Win/Win! When filling out applications, think about what value you would add to the college. Think of college admissions as a two-way street. While colleges are interested in students who will benefit from the range of opportunities that the institute has to offer, colleges also like to brag about the admitted students' profiles, such as their SAT scores, diversity, and number of valedictorians. Good students are their most valuable assets. Therefore, carefully fill out all the parts of your application. Also, being organized is the key ingredient in order to navigate through the process successfully.

1. Request applications. Write letters to the colleges to request applications and other information toward the end of your junior year and no later than the summer between your junior and senior year. Write to more colleges than those to which you plan to apply. For example, if you are planning to apply to six colleges, you may want to request applications from eight colleges just in case you change your mind later. (Reference the sample letter at the end of this chapter.)
2. Photocopy the applications. Make four to five copies of the original applications before you start to fill them out. Practice on these trial applications so that if you are not sure if the essay will fit in the space you can rewrite the essay and adjust accordingly. Once satisfied, fill in the original application.

3. Be neat. Sometimes applications are in the college booklet; Harvard and Yale have such applications. Carefully tear the forms on the perforated lines. Keep your applications neat without crumpling them. Instructions on the application say that you may either type or print clearly. Keep in mind that admissions officers have to read stacks of applications. Handwritten applications can be very hard on their eyes. Imagine an admissions officer reading your application at 11 p.m.—with another fifty applications to go through. It is to your advantage to make it easier on officers by typing your application. With this method, you can have an admission officer's full concentration when he or she reads your application.

4. Read the directions. Carefully read all of the directions and follow all the instructions.

5. Use all of the space wisely. Try to be concise with your answers and fit all of your information in the given space. Do not leave any blank space. By filling the spaces provided in their entirety, you are demonstrating that you have been very thorough in your answers. Try to attempt all of the essay questions, even the optional ones. Admissions officers can gain more insight into who you are with these essays. Admissions officers also tend to value students who have taken the extra time to write them. Writing the optional essay, therefore, shows that you went above and beyond merely satisfying the requirements and that you took the extra time to compose an additional essay.

6. Complete all of the standardized testing scores requests. Make sure that you have all of the required test scores before the application deadline. Before fall of her senior year my daughter had taken the following tests:
   - PSAT
   - SAT I—two attempts
   - SAT II—five different score options from which to choose. (Three SAT II subject test results are required for most admissions)

   If you are organized, it is possible to set attainable goals for fulfilling as many of the test requirements by your junior year as possible. (For details, see chapter 2 on standardized tests.) It is always wise to start early, for you will have the opportunity to retake the test in the fall of the senior year if you feel that any of your scores do not accurately reflect your aptitude.

7. Fill in all of your academic and extracurricular activities. Figure out how to present your
   - Extracurricular activities
   - Academic records
   (See chapter 10 on extracurricular activities for details.)

8. Write your essay. Writing the essay is one of the most time-consuming yet important portions of the application. So, make sure you start early and leave plenty of time for drafts and revisions. (See chapter 11 on the essay for details.)

9. Prepare your recommendation letters. Ask your teachers and guidance counselor to make a copy of your evaluation form. Use this copy as a backup, if needed. Sign a waiver, if appropriate. Submit the two teachers' forms to teachers in two different subject areas. Keep track to see that both teachers' reports were mailed. Ask your counselor or principal to complete the Secondary School Report. (See chapter 12 on recommendation letters and guidance for details.)

10. Locate your high school transcript. The high school transcript is a four-year academic report that reflects your achievements throughout your high school years and consists of two main factors: your grades and your courses. This is usually prepared by your high school counselor and sent along with your guidance evaluation form to the colleges.

11. Keep track of all of the application deadlines. Do not wait for deadlines to mail the application. It is to your advantage to mail your application early. This way it will be read early when there are still plenty of admissions slots open. This advice is especially crucial for applicants facing rolling admissions, as schools process the applications as they arrive.

12. Proofread your work. Proofread your application several times until your points are expressed clearly. All information should be flawless. Have someone such as your friend, teacher, or parent edit your application for grammar, spelling, and mechanics. An editor can be another pair of eyes and can give you constructive criticism, if you wish. When proofreading, walk away from the essay and come back in a few hours or even the next day to make revisions. *Check, check, and recheck* for typos and misspellings. Your application will also be conveying your organizational skills, so meticulously examine your style. You do not want to give admissions officers the wrong impression because of careless spelling and word choice mistakes.

13. Fill out all of the personal information:
    - Name
    - Social security number
    - High school code number

14. Check for your signature. Make sure to sign your application before you mail it.

15. Photocopy the original completed application. Make a copy of the

completed application and use it as a backup in case your original is lost in the mail. You could also use it as a reference in case you have to update any of your information for the college later. Refer to this application to know what was included in the original application.

16. Pay the application fees. Make sure to enclose a check for the application fees.
17. Fill out and mail the postcard. Most applications include a postcard to be filled out by you and mailed with the application. This postcard will be mailed to you later as a written confirmation that the application was received.
18. Fill out and mail financial aid forms.
19. Create and use an official test results and transcripts checklist:
    - Standardized tests: Arrange to have the required (ACT or SAT I and three SAT II subject tests) test results sent directly to the prospective colleges. To organize this process, it helps to make a test score chart, which includes the following:
        - Test names
        - Test dates
        - Test scores
        - Names of the colleges
        - Reminder to release the appropriate test scores to the colleges
    - AP scores: Record all of the AP test scores released to the prospective colleges (see charts).
    - Supplementary transcripts: Keep track of any college or summer school transcripts of credit earned during your high school years that you wish to send to all the colleges (See chart).
20. Create a folder for each college application. On the cover make an application checklist as follows (see chart):
    - Name of the college
    - Application forms (part I and part II)
    - Application deadline (postmarked)
    - Two teacher evaluations
    - Counselor's recommendation
    - Official high school transcripts
    - Application fees
    - Appropriate test scores released
    - Freshman financial aid application
    - Personal alumni interview
    - Miscellaneous
    - Midyear school report
    - Reply date for accepted applicants

21. Create a master college application checklist. It is also useful to have a master checklist of all of the colleges to which you wish to apply. This way, for quick reference you can create an overview of all of your college applications' status at one glance.
    - Names of all of the different colleges to which you wish to apply
    - College applications received/outstanding
    - Early application deadline dates
    - Regular application deadline dates
    - Dates when all the completed parts of the applications are mailed
    - Confirmation from colleges that the application is complete
22. Mail all of the parts of the application at once, if appropriate. Parents can get involved by requesting that the guidance counselor collect all of the teachers' recommendation letters and mail the completed application along with their guidance evaluation form and application fees. Parents can directly give the self-addressed and posted mailing envelope to your guidance counselor (see chapter 12 on recommendation letters).
23. Consider postage. You could send the application regular mail if you have enough time. However, we always found it beneficial to mail all of the applications, even the ones that were sent out early, by priority mail, and we paid extra to keep track of the postage and to receive return confirmation. With this choice, we had a written receipt for our records.
24. Call the college. Two weeks after you have mailed your application, you should call the college and get a confirmation that the application is complete and that the school has received all of your materials, including your test scores. Make a note of the date and time and the person to whom you spoke in the admissions office regarding your application, especially if he or she confirms that the application is complete. If the recommendation letters were mailed separately, make sure they are mailed before the application deadline. Some colleges mail postcards confirming that all parts of the application were received.
25. Compose thank-you notes. Write thank-you notes to all of your teachers who wrote your recommendation letters and helped you with application essay corrections. Also send thank-you notes to anyone who assisted you with the proofreading or typing of the application.

IMPORTANT POINTS TO REMEMBER

1. Write to all the colleges to request the application form.
2. Write to more colleges than those to which you plan to apply. For

example, if you are planning to apply to six colleges, you may want to request applications from eight colleges just in case you change your mind later.

3. Keep track of all of the received applications.
4. Make four to five copies of the original application before you start filling them out. Practice on these applications first.
5. Carefully read all of the directions.
6. Use space wisely and try to fit all of your information in the given space.
7. Be neat.
8. Fill out all of the personal information.
   - Name
   - Social security number
   - High school code
9. Application Completion Checklist:
   - Complete all of the forms.
   - Fill in your extracurricular achievements.
   - Complete the academic records.
   - Write your personal commentary (essay).
   - Sign waiver, if appropriate, on recommendation forms.
   - Submit the two teachers' forms to teachers in two different subjects.
   - Keep track to see that both teachers' recommendations were mailed.
   - Ask your counselor or principal to complete your secondary school report.
   - Check to see if your high school transcript has been mailed.
   - Request that the Educational Testing Service release the appropriate test results.
   - Sign your application.
10. Send AP test results, if applicable.
11. Proofread your completed application.
12. Keep track of application deadlines.
13. Send freshman year financial aid application, if appropriate.
14. Send application fees.
15. Make a copy of your completed application for your own records before mailing it to the institution. Use it as a backup, if needed.
16. Mail your application.
17. Make sure that the college has received all of the parts of your application.
18. Keep track of your mid-term school report and the date when it should be returned.
19. Keep track of the reply date on accepted applications.

SAMPLE LETTER TO REQUEST APPLICATIONS

Street Address
City, State, Zip
Date

Director of Admissions
Name of College/ University
Address

Dear Admissions Officer:

I will be a senior at [name of high school] in the fall of [year] and am interested in knowing more about college/university. I would appreciate you sending me the following:

1. Application for admission
2. Information such as college costs, course catalogs, and other pertinent bulletins
3. Information related to your interests; for example, you may request information about the band, field hockey, debate societies, and so on
4. Financial aid information [if needed]

Sincerely,

Your signature

Full name

APPLICATION CHECKLIST

Name of the college _____

- ☐ Application forms (part I and part II)
- ☐ Application deadline (postmarked)
- ☐ Two teacher evaluations
- ☐ Counselor's recommendation
- ☐ Official high school transcripts
- ☐ Application fees
- ☐ Appropriate test scores released
- ☐ Freshman financial aid application
- ☐ Personal alumni interview
- ☐ Miscellaneous
- ☐ Midyear school report
- ☐ Reply date for accepted applicants

APPLICATION TIMETABLE

Name of the college _____

☐ Part I application	mailed on	_____
☐ Part II application	mailed on	_____
☐ Application fees	mailed on	_____
☐ First teacher's recommendation	mailed on	_____
☐ Second teacher's recommendation	mailed on	_____
☐ Counselor's recommendation	mailed on	_____
☐ Official school transcript	mailed on	_____
☐ Other transcripts (summer/college)	mailed on	_____
☐ SAT I/ACT scores	sent on	_____
☐ SAT II scores	sent on	_____
☐ AP scores	sent on	_____
☐ Confirmation of complete application	received on	_____
☐ Letter of acceptance/denial/wait	received on	_____
☐ Letter of acceptance reply (to enroll)	received on	_____
☐ Wait list reply	sent on	_____

APPLICATION CHART

Name of the college _____

Application

Date application form sent _____   Application fee sent _____

Letters of recommendation

First teacher recommendation

Name of teacher _____   Date letter of recommendation mailed _____

Teacher recommendation received by college _____

Second teacher recommendation

Name of teacher _____   Date letter of recommendation mailed _____

Teacher recommendation received by college _____

Outside recommendations

Guidance counselor _____   Guidance counselor report mailed _____

Guidance counselor report received by college _____

High school transcript mailed _____

Other transcripts (summer schools, colleges) mailed _____

Midyear school report given _____

Midyear school report received by college _____

Test scores

SAT I scores released _____   ACT scores released _____

SAT II scores (list specific subject areas) released _____

AP exams (list specific subject areas) released _____

NINE

Early Decision and Early Action

Some colleges' admissions policies are early action (EA), while others are early decision (ED). Carefully review all of your college applications to find out each college's policies regarding its early decision or early action programs. Candidates apply for early decision by a certain application deadline, which is usually around the first or second week of November and are not permitted to apply to any other college through the early decision or early action program. Once again, review all of the literature to find out the specific application deadlines for various colleges. Focus on the colleges that you are strongly considering for early decision or early action.

To be eligible for early decision or early action, you should complete all testing requirements usually by the November test dates. However, it is strongly suggested that you complete your standardized tests by October. Students choosing "early action will need to plan their testing schedule accordingly (and preferably complete their testing by the October series, although November tests normally arrive on time)" (Harvard University, *Harvard for Entrance*, 2).

Since the early decision program is binding, it is suited for those students who are confident in determining their first choice of a college. You cannot apply to more than one college for early decision. Most binding early decision applications require students to agree in writing not to apply anywhere else. Some colleges even request a counselor's signature to ensure that the student is applying only to one college for early decision. If admitted to a school through early decision, you will be required to withdraw applications from all other colleges.

In contrast, candidates applying to nonbinding early action programs may apply to other institutions with similar programs. (However, applicants must still comply with these colleges' policies.) Unlike the early decision programs, which are binding, early action programs give students more flexibility. My daughter applied to nonbinding early programs offered by Harvard, MIT, and Georgetown. Once she was admitted to these colleges, she was not forced to withdraw her regular decision application from other colleges. Her options were open, and application deadlines did not force her to make a hasty and ill-informed choice.

Around mid-December, candidates will be notified if they are classified as accepted (admitted to the institution), denied, or deferred for admission. Deferred candidates will be considered again for admission in the regular decision pool. During the regular decision application process, deferred applicants will be either denied or admitted. Observation suggests that most likely these students will not be placed on the waiting list. If a candidate is offered admission under the early decision policy, he or she must reply around the first week of February. However, a candidate who is admitted to a nonbinding early action program has until the first week of May to decide whether to accept or decline. These options make EA an attractive choice. Applicants who are looking for a way to enhance their chance of getting into an Ivy League school may choose to apply either early decision or early action.

Students often use the strategy of applying for either early decision or early action because they think that they may have a greater chance for acceptance since most colleges admit a higher percentage of applicants under these programs. But one of the reasons for such a high admission rate is that the application pool in some of the highly selective colleges is very strong. These students are highly motivated and academically stronger. According to Harvard University admissions, "There is no strategic advantage to applying to Harvard Early Action. The higher acceptance rate under our early action program reflects the remarkable strength of this self-selected application pool" (Harvard University, *Introduction*, 48).

Based on these standards, if you have average grades that do not stand out in the regular admission applicant pool, do not require financial aid, and if you are sure that the school is your first choice, ED may be a good strategy but also a gamble. For example, my nephew wanted to apply early either to Harvard or Yale, but based on his admission profile, his counselor strongly suggested that he apply to Cornell. His counselor's experience in dealing with the admissions staff of all selective schools suggested that Cornell would be more likely than any other Ivy League school to accept him. He did get into Cornell (binding early decision program), but he always regretted not trying for Yale. On the other hand, some other students who had similar profiles did not take the counselor's advice of applying to appropriately suited colleges for early decision, and in the event they did not get into any highly selective colleges for early or regular decision. Surprisingly, one of these students was the valedictorian of his class.

In conclusion, early action or early decision may be a good strategy for those candidates whose records have been consistently strong over time.

However, the regular decision path is surely a favorable option for those applicants whose admission profile will be improved significantly by senior year extracurricular achievements, improved academic performance, and maybe additional test scores to strengthen their academic qualifications.

IMPORTANT POINTS TO REMEMBER

Early Decision versus Early Action

EARLY DECISION

1. Early decision simply means that if you apply to a college for early decision and are accepted to that institution then you must attend.
2. Once admitted, you must withdraw your applications from all of the other colleges to which you have already applied, for early decision admission is binding.
3. The applicant pool in highly selective colleges for early decision students is usually stronger than that for regular decision.
4. There are a few advantages to applying for early decision. Early decision indicates to your prospective colleges that you're seriously interested in that college and it is your first choice. Also, if you are indeed admitted early you can cut back on the costly application fees and the time-consuming pressure of completing several applications.
5. The disadvantage to early decision is that the commitment is binding, forcing the candidate to enroll at that college. Also, you may only apply to one college for early decision, making this choice a difficult one.
6. Another pitfall concerns financial aid. Early decision applicants have only one offer instead of several extremely negotiable offers from various colleges. As mentioned by Edward B. Fiske, "Another hidden motive for financially strapped colleges is the fact that most ED applicants tend to be from upper-income brackets. . . . Most colleges jump at the chance to lock in ED students who will not need financial aid" (Fiske, 138).

EARLY ACTION

1. If you apply to a college early action and you are accepted, you do not have to commit to that college until around the first of May, depending on the individual college's deadlines.

2. This option allows you to apply to more than one college. (Some colleges, such as Brown, MIT, Georgetown, and Harvard allowed students to apply to more than one college for early action in 2000.)
3. The application pool for the early action program is usually stronger than the regular decision program for most highly selective colleges. The same pool may apply to more than one early action college, making the competition fiercer than that for early decision.
4. There are advantages to knowing that you are admitted to any early action program. You at least have a college to fall back on and might apply to fewer colleges on regular decision. Also, you are not committed to attend that school. If you are accepted to a preferable college in regular decision, you can change your mind.

Advice for Both Approaches

1. When applying either early decision or early action, make sure you have completed the required entrance testing (including the SAT I and SAT II) before the start of your senior year. (The latest October testing date of your senior year is preferable.) If you are organized, you will have all testing completed by the end of your junior year. This plan would add to the quality of your application for highly selective colleges.
2. When you apply ED or EA, you will be notified around mid-December whether you are accepted, deferred (meaning your application will be placed among the regular decision pool to be considered once again), or rejected.
3. If deferred, call the college to find out if you need to send admissions any additional information.

Deadlines

1. Deadlines for both ED and EA are usually in the second week of November. The earlier you mail your application, the better. Read all of the application instructions carefully for details concerning your tentative choice.
2. The colleges usually make their decisions by mid-December. Again, always check with the college for exact dates.

TEN

Extracurricular Activities

Admissions for Harvard's class of 2004 rejected from their applicant pool one thousand valedictorians and two hundred students who had perfect SAT scores. Marlyn McGrath Lewis, Harvard's director of admissions, notes in the *Kaplan Newsweek 2001 edition* of *How to Get into College* that "what you need is something to make you stand out in the face of daunting competition. The surging number of baby-boomlet kids graduating from high school has created a bumper crop of overqualified applicants" (King, 38). At highly selective colleges, things like your extracurricular achievements can have strategic significance. By participating in extracurricular activities, you can boost your chances of admission to the colleges of your choice. As mentioned by Rochelle Sharpe in the *Wall Street Journal*: "The change comes as extracurricular activities are already playing a growing role in both the admissions process and the awarding of scholarships. In an era of rampant grade inflation and standardized-test tutoring, colleges say it's getting harder to pinpoint superstars based on grades and scores alone. So as acceptance letters get delivered this month, extracurricular activities are a bigger factor than ever in deciding who gets the celebrated thick envelope" (W1). Most colleges are interested in applicants who can positively contribute to their student community by actively pursuing their established interests. The admissions process is your opportunity to market and present the best portrait of yourself to the admissions officers. College consultant Mary Clarke notes, "You have to have a passion. If you collect butterflies go out and do it" (King, 37).

To build this individual portrait, students should not be afraid to be creative and to pursue their passions through extracurricular activities. Following the wise saying that well begun is half done, the best approach to finding your true passions is to explore activities as early as possible. Without attempting to find your passion, you may find yourself randomly enrolling in a myriad of activities without having any real commitment. The earlier you begin your participation in the chosen activity, the sooner you will learn about your strengths, weaknesses, likes, and dislikes and thus be able to pursue the goals that are most meaningful to you. The earlier you commit to an activity, the better your chances are of rising from a group member to a leader, thus allowing yourself to include such noteworthy accomplishments and activities on your application. If you do not start early, you will find yourself in a position in your senior year where all activities seem to offer the same benefits. Your choice between including varsity or junior varsity tennis in your schedule in order to build your application profile without first finding out if you will qualify to make the team will not produce any satisfactory results.

In our experiences, we encouraged our kids to explore as many activities as possible starting in the ninth grade. Based on their interests, they pursued the prospects that were most meaningful to them. They modified their lists by examining the time that they had to devote to these activities. We made sure they gave at least two to four years of commitment to each activity.

To ease the stress of the application process, Vinay and Sheila created an activities journal in the ninth grade in which they recorded all of their activities, big or small. They also recorded the number of hours committed to each activity and noted any significant contributions that they made to these activities, mentioning any awards, honors, or distinctions achieved. It is very crucial to note all of the details when the experience is fresh in your mind. If it is difficult to remember participating in an activity a month after it has occurred, imagine recalling activities three years later when it is time to fill out college applications.

Juggling schoolwork, participating in extracurricular activities, and completing college applications can be a grueling experience for students. As filling out each application takes a lot of their time, it is inevitable that their efforts can easily be diluted. For example, my son overlooked mentioning participating in an extracurricular activity that may have enhanced his application. As we came to understand how puzzling and demanding completing these applications could be, we learned from experience and were motivated to have a jump start in the process for my daughter.

In the summer between her junior and senior year, Sheila did her best to figure out how to rank all of her extracurricular activities and academic awards. She referred to it later when filling out her applications. Organizing your approach for adding these qualifications to your applications not only helps you go through the admission process efficiently, it also significantly improves your chances over other applicants simply by focusing your attention on application details.

To achieve this focus, students must stress quality over quantity. For most admissions officers, the quality of a student's commitment to one activity is more valued than the number of activities (with no commitment) in which he or she is involved. Usually, the trends of in-depth commitment are quite evident. Doing volunteer work with minimal commitment of less than one hour per week for fewer than five weeks does nothing to enhance the application and we felt was not worth mentioning. As noted by Michele A. Hernández, who was Dartmouth's admission officer and author of the book *A Is for Admission*, "One church-mission trip or serving soup to the homeless for an hour on Fridays is not going to help your chance for admission" (114). When my son included activities such as these, it took away from his other activities and made his extracurricular profile look like a laundry list of activities. It was not necessary for Vinay to be involved with too many insignificant leadership roles, such as French Club, where the commitment to these activities is trivial in most schools. Listing these activities took away from his other more noteworthy leadership roles such as class president, president of the National Honor Society, and most valuable player and team captain for varsity tennis.

There are extracurricular achievements, moreover, that can actually detract from your application image. Including activities with negligible involvement such as a one-time effort in helping to organize a teacher's appreciation lunch can actually work against you. Being selective with meaningful activities is far more impressive than including a laundry list. Admissions officers would rather see students' passions and deep convictions in their commitments. According to Lee Stetson, the University of Pennsylvania's dean of admissions, "We realized one of the better predictors of success is the ability to dedicate oneself to a task and do it well" (Sharpe, W1). This level of dedication reflects on the applicant as someone who would enrich the student body.

Highly selective colleges are looking for evidence of initiative and held leadership positions. The earlier you begin your selective participation, the better your chances are for finding success within this area. My son started as a member of the tennis team and rose to be captain by his senior year. My daughter started as an amateur cross-country runner in ninth grade, and her team was state qualified during her senior year. Both of them were able to use these achievements and developments on their applications. Admissions officers can identify traits like motivation and initiative by an applicants' commitment toward their extracurricular activities—traits that standardized tests and the academic profile, for example, cannot measure. My son's devotion to tennis showed these traits. Additionally, admissions officers consider any state or regional recognition a remarkable commitment, as with my daughter's accomplishments on the cross-country team.

However, I cautioned my kids not to do anything just to impress the admissions officers or us. It was very important that they enjoyed what they were involved in and that they never came across as programmed or bored with an activity. Officers can recognize this. We encouraged our kids to follow their dreams and find their own passion for whatever they liked to do. The evidence of their commitment is also displayed in one of their essays. (See chapter 11 on the essay for details.)

In order to build your applications and your profile, long-term commitment in an activity is greatly preferred to participating in several meaningless activities. Since my daughter concentrated on only a few activities, she was able to give her utmost commitment to them and still have sufficient time to concentrate on academics. Not only did this choice give her the opportunity to present her activities in an outstanding manner, but it also allowed the application to stand out in the face of daunting competition.

One of the best times to explore some of these activities was in the summer, when my kids could extend their commitment from the school to the community. They also discovered that it is a good idea to get involved with some volunteer work in the summer, to get a job, or to try both. During her four years of high school, Sheila had various summer experiences such as working at the Gap, volunteering at the local Community Foundation of the Eastern Shore, and attending summer school. Vinay, on the other hand, volunteered at the hospital, took some summer courses, and held various summer jobs.

Based on her personal experience, my daughter has compiled the following useful advice for those compiling their extracurricular activity descriptions:

1. Explore many activities during the first year of high school.
2. Continue participation in the choices that are meaningful to you.
3. Involve yourself in a few activities and maintain an in-depth commitment.
4. Maintain an activity journal, recording the number of hours committed.
5. Record any significant contribution received in any activity.
6. Show evidence of motivation and initiation in your activity.
7. Rise to leadership positions progressively throughout your high school career.
8. Plan to commit for at least two to four years in each activity.
9. Experience suggests that value comes not with quantity but with quality of commitment to these activities.
10. Mention activities that you were involved in during high school only.
11. Consider also volunteering in your community.

COMPILING YOUR LIST OF ACTIVITIES

1. Begin to compile your list of activities in the summer of your junior year. List all the activities, significant and insignificant, in which

you were involved, starting with ninth grade. Then go back and fine-tune your list.

2. When listing activities, mention any leadership roles you held, important responsibilities you had, or any major accomplishments achieved by the organization while you were a member or participant.
3. Specify the number of hours you spent per week doing the activity.
4. Rank the list of activities from most to least important and from present (twelfth grade) to past (ninth grade).
5. When deciding what activities to list, first identify those in which you received national or state recognition or in which you had a big role or made a major impact.

Table 10.1. An Example of Sheila's Extracurricular Activity List

Activity	Position Held	Grades Participated	Hours per Week/ Weeks per Year
Youth Foundation Fund of the Community Foundation of the Eastern Shore	Founder/chair	11, 12	5/18
Girl Scouts	Gold Award, 1999 Leadership Award, 1998 Challenge Award, 1997–1998	9, 10, 11, 12	3/15
Mock Trial	Team captain; voted all-star; earned pin (9th); qualified regional competition, ranked top 8 in state	9, 10, 11, 12	12/20
Cross-Country	Earned varsity letter (9th); earned pin (10th–12th); qualified regional competition	9, 10, 11, 12	20/36
Student Government	Freshman/sophomore class president; special events SGA chair (11th); nominated to attend leadership symposiums at Salisbury State University (9th–12th)	9, 10, 11, 12	2–10/40
Maryland Food Bank	Canned food drives	9, 10, 11, 12	0–10/40
Church/Temple		9, 10, 11, 12	2–8/52

Colleges may ask you to list your work experience and academic honors separately. If so, follow a similar format. Remember to be concise and to elaborate on those activities that may be unfamiliar to the college admissions officers reading your application. Examples of both are provided below.

Table 10.2. An Example of Sheila's Work Experience List

Specific Nature of Work	Employer	Dates of Employment	Hours per Week
Sales associate	Gap, Inc.	Summer 1998, Summer 1999	15
Administrative intern	Community Foundation of the Eastern Shore	Summer 1999	15
Intern	United States Senator Paul Sarbanes	Fall 1999	0–3

ACADEMIC HONORS

Grade 12: National Merit Commended Scholar
- National Honor Society (elected president)
- Honor Roll
- Nominated to serve on the Secondary Education Advisory Committee for the Wicomico County Board of Education (one nominee per school)
- French Honor Society (elected vice president)
- Mu Alpha Theta

Grade 11: National Honor Society (earned Lamp of Knowledge pin)
- Honor Roll
- French Honor Society (elected secretary)
- Mu Alpha Theta
- Chosen to participate in Junior Science and Humanities Symposium at the University of Maryland (two selected per school)
- Selected to participate in Summer Engineering Program at the University of Maryland (sixty women selected nationwide)
- Student of the Month (French)
- Service Award
- Minds in Motion Award

Grade 10: National Honor Society (earned academic letter)
- French Honor Society
- Mu Alpha Theta
- Service Award
- Minds in Motion Award

Grade 9: Honor Roll
- French Honor Society
- Mu Alpha Theta
- Junior Varsity Math Team (second place in Wicomico County)
- Student of the Month (English)
- Service Award
- Minds in Motion Award
- Optimist Oratorical Contest (first place, zone contest; first place, district contest; contender in state contest).

OTHER TIPS

1. When listing activities, emphasize accomplishments for each activity.
2. Each college may have a slightly different format, but if you compile a list of activities similar to these examples you will speed up the application process when you have to list your activities, honors, and work experience.
3. Make sure to carefully consider each activity you place on your list. Here are some useful examples demonstrating the difference between an impressive and an unimpressive accomplishment.

Impressive activities:

- Student government, particularly leadership roles
- Editor of school newspaper
- Girl Scout Gold Award
- Eagle Scout award
- Founder of a club
- Any state or national recognition

Unimpressive activities:

- Member of strawberry club
- Volunteer for teacher's appreciation lunch (with only three hours and a one-time participation)
- Dance committee member
- One-week tennis camp

IMPORTANT POINTS TO REMEMBER

1. Explore the range of activities available in your high school.
2. Join as many activities as possible that you would like to explore in your freshman year.

3. Follow your dreams and find your passion in your extracurricular activities.
4. Admissions officers would rather see your passion and deep conviction in your commitment to what you most value and not in your volume of extracurricular achievements.
5. Modify your list of activities based on the amount of time you have for these activities. Pursue the ones that are most meaningful to you.
6. Being selective with meaningful activities is far more impressive than including a laundry list.
7. Commit at least two to four years to each activity.
8. Consider exploring clubs and academic honor societies in your school.
9. Create an activity journal as early as ninth grade for all of your participation in extracurricular activities. Keep track of the following:
   - Number of hours
   - Number of days per week
   - Number of weeks per year
   - Any significant contributions made to these activities
10. Think about exploring a range of summer extracurricular activities or volunteer work.
11. Reflect on extending your participation to outside of your school and into your community.
12. Show evidence of initiative toward your activities in the progressive years of involvement.
13. Assume leadership roles in your junior and senior year, if appropriate.
14. Mention your participation for high school years only.
15. Remember how to precisely rank your list of activities that you would like to record on your application.
   - Jump-start the process in the summer after your junior year.
   - Organize on a rough draft.
   - Begin compiling the activities/academic awards list.
   - Mention any award, honors, or distinction earned during these years.
   - Rank in the order of importance to you.
   - Rank according to progressive grades.
   - Refer to this rough draft when filling out the actual application.
16. Be concise, but make sure to elaborate on the activities where you have a significant contribution and where you want the admissions officers to notice.
17. When filling out your college applications, refer to your notes in your activity journal to make sure that you have included all of your activities.

ELEVEN

The Essay

WHAT YOUR ESSAY REVEALS

Almost all applications from selective colleges will ask you to write at least one essay. Admissions officers can get a profile of your academic side from your test scores and GPA, and this information is available in your application. However, essays help admissions officers understand your personal side, giving the readers a glimpse of who you really are, how you think, and what's special or unique about you. You should allow your personality to shine through your essay. Write about your personal experience as if it were a good short story that you take pleasure in telling.

Also, when admissions officers read your essay, they are not only learning another side of you, but they are also seeing how well you write. The application essay allows you to demonstrate your writing ability. Keep this list in mind when writing your essay:

1. Be grammatically precise.
2. Use well-structured sentences.
3. Write a well-organized essay with an opening (introduction), middle (body), and ending (conclusion).
4. Make sure that when your sentences and paragraphs are put together, they flow well and have smooth transitions. You want to keep the central idea of your essay clear.
   [Sheila's experience suggest the following useful tips.]

TIPS FOR WRITING THE ESSAY

1. Start as early as possible. The earlier you start writing your essay, the more time you will have to write and rewrite your prose without worrying about deadlines. You will even have the luxury of walking away from your final draft and reviewing it after a few

91

days, with a fresh mind. This distance allows you to view your work objectively, for writers need to see their product from the reader's perspective in order to assess its ability to communicate to the designated audience.

2. Carefully choose a topic.
   • List several essay topics.
   • Read the essay question carefully and familiarize yourself with the difficult topics.
   • Make some key points for each topic.
   • Choose a topic that you enjoy and feel strongly about.
   • Choose a topic that has the most potential for you, enabling you to incorporate insights into who you are, what's unique about you, or how you think.

3. Outline what you want to include.
   • Brainstorm different ideas you wish to include in your essay.
   • List everything, significant or insignificant, that you can think of.
   • Review your list and start narrowing your options, deciding what you want to include or to eliminate.
   • Go over the list, highlighting the key points that could be the main idea for your essay.
   • When answering broad-based questions such as those asking you to state a significant experience, try to choose something that is a big part of your life or an event that you view as important.
   • Write about what you think is important; do not try to impress admissions officers by writing about what you think they will find interesting. Do not write, for example, about how you wish to save the children and then have nothing in your essay or in your list of extracurricular activities to support how you tried to accomplish this goal. The bottom line is you should not have an idealistic essay. Instead, be honest! Most readers will be impressed with your true accomplishments rather than with superficial statements that they have likely read many times before.

4. Write your first draft. Refer to the main points on your outline. Be in charge of your essay; build up a story you enjoy telling a close friend, and try keeping the narrative like a conversation that naturally flows. Admissions officers want to know what is special about you. Use this opportunity to compose the best prose and let your personality be the focus of the writing. Pay close attention to content and make sure that you stay within the assigned topic. Use vivid, descriptive language. Remember this is only your rough draft. Here are some useful tips to keep in mind:
   • Be original! Your topic may not necessarily have to be original, but your approach should.

- Do not use clichés. Clichés demonstrate a lack of imagination and originality in your writing skills. They do not give the reader an accurate description of the event or person that you are individually expressing.
- Do not over quote. Using too many quotes in your essay takes away from expressing real events and experiences in detail and in your own words. The essay also becomes too choppy to read.
- Keep the essay simple. Do not use every new word you learned for the SAT.
- Make sure you answer the question. Look back to the original essay topic during and after you have written the essay to make sure you are answering the question asked of you.

5. Look at the purpose of your opening paragraph.
   - Compose an interesting introduction. Use your first line as an attention grabber, or hook. You can do this through hyperbole, as one specific strategy. (See, for example, the mention of four thousand peanut butter and jelly sandwiches in the Community Foundation essay at the end of this chapter.)
   - In my cross-country essay, I started off with a vivid description of the setting of my experience with which I was able to draw the reader directly into my narrative.
   - Another approach could be starting with a rhetorical question that is appropriate to your topic.
   - Think of lots of different approaches that work for your topic. Remember the essay's purpose when brainstorming these approaches, as your introduction must match the form and tone of the rest of the piece.

6. Critically evaluate what you have written.
   - Stick to the assigned essay topic. Make sure you answer the question asked of you when writing the essay. Make sure your essay has a point!
   - Make one point in your essay and use that as your center of focus. For example, suppose you are trying to convey to the admissions officers that one of your personal qualities is determination. Instead of directly stating that you are a determined person, demonstrate this quality in your essay. (See the cross-country essay below for a specific example.)
   - Let your personality shine. This is your chance to show the admissions officers who you are beyond the grades and the numbers. If your essay does not project a true portrait of yourself as you would like it to, add more examples and details in order to make the essay more descriptive.
   - Be yourself. Admissions officers are also looking for sensitivity

and conviction in your essay. Explain your weaknesses or vulnerabilities, and express truth and honesty in your essay. A passion for whatever you discuss, no matter how big or small, should be apparent. For example, in my essay about running cross-country, I went one step beyond what was expected of the writing by explaining why I truly love the sport.

- Be positive. While it is acceptable to explain your weaknesses, do not be negative; show your strengths as well. Maintain a positive attitude in your essay. This expression will be indicative of your personality and create a great essay.

7. Modify and compose a final draft.

- Keep your essay like a conversation. The essay should flow easily and leave the reader knowing a little more about you (with things that cannot be portrayed in a transcript). The essay should leave the reader wanting to learn more about you or even wanting to meet you.
- Share your personal experiences. These instances provide the reader with insight into some of your personal and unique qualities. They reflect your whole personality, including your values, goals, and sense of humor. After you have written your essay, you can ask a friend or family member to read the essay to make sure it is correctly portraying your personality. Also, an additional reader can help you to check the flow and style of your writing.
- While outside assistance is helpful, do not let others (especially Mom and Dad) write the essay for you. Your parents can help you with your essay, but do not let them influence you too much with their adult thinking. Admissions officers can easily spot this. After all, this is your time to have a conversation with the admissions officers.
- The essay should tell a story. Begin with a clear introduction and then logically connect the body paragraphs to ultimately end with some sort of conclusion or resolution.
- End with a strong conclusion that ties the essay together. This paragraph is the last thought you leave your readers, so end with a strong impression. You might wish to consider ending with a question, a prediction, or a determination that connects to your experiences.
- Avoid ending the essay with statements such as "The moral of my experience was _____." Announcements suggest that the reader cannot infer for him or herself the point that you wish to make within the piece.

8. Edit your final draft. This time, check all of the technicalities of the

essay instead of the content. Thoroughly review the following elements:

- Spelling
- Grammar
- Sentence structure
- Smoothly flowing transitions
- Style and overall tone of the essay
- Neatness

9. Proofread your final copy. Proofread your paper several times until your points are expressed clearly and the essay flows well. Use transitions to aid in keeping the paper interesting and coherent. Have an English teacher proofread your essay as well for grammar and spelling, all of which should be flawless. When proofreading yourself, walk away from the essay and come back in a few hours or even the next day to make revisions

10. Check, check, and recheck for typos and misspellings. Your essay will also be conveying your writing style, and you do not want to give admissions officers the wrong impression because of careless spelling mistakes.

11. Make sure that the essay is within the designated word limit. The piece can go over by a little or you can even attach a separate sheet of paper if the space provided is insufficient, but do not go overboard and overburden the admissions readers by attaching too many pages and making your essay too long. When attaching separate sheets of paper, label the top of each attached sheet with your name, social security number, and the essay topic. A few helpful tips to fit a long essay in the space provided:

- Reduce the font size to 11.
- Reduce the top and the bottom margins.
- Reduce from double spacing to 1.5 line space.
- Reduce side margins.

12. Look at the final details. Read the essay with a fresh mind. Does it give a snapshot of your true personality? Does it convey an accurate impression of you to the admissions officers? Make sure to write your name and social security number on the essay. Show the essay to an English teacher, parent, outside helper, or anyone who can honestly give you constructive criticism and feedback.

POSSIBLE ESSAY TOPICS

Colleges usually ask you to write one essay describing a personal experience that has had a significant impact on your life. Other questions in-

quire about sports or other extracurricular activities that have been meaningful to you and why so. These two topics are standard, and by knowing
this ahead of time you can start working on your essay early, even before
you receive your application. Past essay topics, all from 1999–2000 application forms, have included:

1. Please relate your interest in studying at Georgetown University to
   your future goals. How do these thoughts relate to your chosen
   course of study? (Georgetown University)
2. Evaluate a significant experience, achievement, or risk that you
   have taken and its impact on you. (Harvard University)
3. Discuss some issue of personal, local, national, or international concern and its importance to you. (Harvard University)
4. Indicate a person who has had a significant influence on you, and
   describe that influence. (Harvard University)
5. Describe a character in fiction, a historical figure, or a creative work
   (as in art, music, science, etc.) that has had an influence on you, and
   explain that influence. (Harvard University)
6. Please write an essay about an activity or interest that has been particularly meaningful to you. (Yale University)
7. Why do you consider Duke a good match for you? Is there something in particular you anticipate contributing to the Duke community? (Duke University)
8. Consider the books you have read in the last year or two either for
   school or for leisure. Please discuss the way in which one of them
   changed your understanding of the world, other people, or yourself. (Duke University)
9. What one class, teacher, book, or experience can you point to as
   having really *changed the way you think*? Explain. (Princeton University)
10. Discuss something *(anything)* you just wished you understood bet-
    ter. (Princeton University)
11. If you could hold one position, elected or appointed, in government
    (at any level), which one would you want it to be, and why?
    (Princeton University)
12. What one or two suggestions would you have if asked about how
    we might improve race relations in this country or around the
    world? (Princeton University)
13. What work of art, music, science, mathematics, or literature has
    surprised or unsettled or changed you, and in what way? (Univer-
    sity of Virginia)

14. Make a bold prediction about something in the year 2020 that no one else has made a bold prediction about. (University of Virginia)

15. If you could cause any one living person to change his or her mind about one thing, whom would you pick, and how would you change his or her thinking? (University of Virginia)

16. "The past isn't dead. It's not even past." So says the lawyer Gavin Stevens near the end of Faulkner's *Requiem for a Nun*. To borrow Stevens' words, what small event, either from your personal history or the history of the world, is neither "dead" nor "past"? (University of Virginia)

17. Does *discrimination* still exist? What single experience or event has led to your conclusion? (University of Virginia)

18. What is your favorite word, and why? (University of Virginia)

19. Please describe your intellectual interests, their evolution, and what makes them exciting to you. (Cornell University)

20. In 100 words or less describe your most important academic accomplishment or intellectual experience to date. We don't want to know about test scores or course grades, rather we want to know about your creativity, your willingness to take intellectual risks or your affinity for scholarly endeavors. (Massachusetts Institute of Technology)

21. In 100 words or less describe your most important *non-academic* activity and why it is important to you. (Massachusetts Institute of Technology)

22. Tell us about an opinion that you have had to defend or an incident in your life which placed you in conflict with the beliefs of a majority of people and explain how this affected your value system. (Massachusetts Institute of Technology)

23. Your personal values and strongly held opinions are usually set at an early age. Describe how you have come to question some of these values and opinions. How did *you* change as a result of your shift in values? (University of Maryland, College Park)

24. Think back over the past three years. What has been the most important *academic* experience you have had? Describe why you think it was such an important experience in your growth as a student. (University of Maryland, College Park)

25. Describe the most important experience with adversity you have encountered. Tell us about *how* you responded, coped, or triumphed. The seriousness of the adversity is less important than the thoughtfulness with which you describe how you responded and what you think you learned. (University of Maryland, College Park)

SAMPLE ESSAYS

The following are some of Sheila's college essays. These will hopefully provide you with further insight on how to approach the essay portion of the application. It is important to note that unlike essays written for an English class in high school, these essays, while they maintain proper grammar, punctuation, and the like, are more like conversations. Some of the following essays were written as optional essays. If given a choice to write optional essays for a college, you should take the opportunity. Admissions officers can gain more insight into who you are with these essays. Admissions officers also tend to value students who have gone beyond merely satisfying the requirements and taken the extra time to write them. For some colleges, writing the optional essay may mean writing an entirely new essay, which may require more time and planning on your part. But for other colleges, the optional essay may just ask you to include anything else that you may not have previously mentioned in the application. With this type of open-ended question, you can easily submit another essay that you perhaps had previously written for another college.

Community Foundation (Harvard Optional Essay)

I set out to save the world, and I soon discovered what a hard task it was going to be. Four thousand peanut butter and jelly sandwiches and one thousand switch plates later with the completion of my Girl Scout Gold Award project, I found my passion. I have done a lot of volunteer work, but I have always felt I should do something more. I attend a rural public high school with a diverse student body. Recently, I noticed divisions in the classroom that I had never seen before and all because of a Six Flags field trip. Some of my classmates neglected to turn in their permission slips. This was a quiet way for them to announce that they could not afford to go. I took a step back and realized how many things my friends and I take for granted.

Seeking to help, I thought about creating a program to raise money for high school students. From SAT prep programs to leadership conferences, I found myself drawing up a list of activities that every student should have an opportunity to participate in. I began talking to lawyers and CPAs to determine how to turn my dream into reality. But I soon discovered how difficult it can be to accomplish anything in the "adult world." I ran into legal requirements, such as getting an IRS tax-exempt code. I thought I had come up with an ingenious way to help people, and I naively thought people would be falling over to help me. I soon faced the reality that not everyone would be as enthusiastic about this project as I was. After becoming aware of the Community Foundation of the Eastern

Shore, I met with the executive and assistant directors who became my mentors. They took me through the steps of converting my project from an idea into a founding document and finally into an established Foundation Fund.

As the summer progressed, it was time to hold our first Advisory Committee meeting. I had decided to recruit members based on the nominations of high school principals. My problems soon transformed from recruiting members, learning Excel, and forming a mission statement to anticipating how many pizzas to order. I was quite apprehensive about the meeting. This would be the first time I would get a student response to my idea. Despite my anxiety, the meeting was a huge success! Energized by the ideas generated by the committee, I recognized the power of my plan. I recognized that my idea both could and would come to fruition.

I realize now that I am touching people, that I am making a difference, and that it is worth every hour I have spent with this project. This has been the most exhaustive yet gratifying experience of my life. I have learned tools in the workplace, the importance of teamwork; but most importantly, I have learned more about myself. I was so ready to throw my hands up when lawyers told me that I could not, as a child, create something like this or when a principal trivialized my ideas and seemed uninterested. I waited it out and I am so glad I did because as a result of this one project, I am making a difference. And even if I could help pay for just one more student to go on a Six Flags field trip, I would work so that they could have that opportunity. There were times when I felt like Don Quixote tilting at windmills with no Sancho Panza by my side. But the times when I felt supported and the times when I knew others were envisioning my dream always outweighed the bad. I set out to save the world and what a great world it is to save.

Cross-Country Essay

The rustling of leaves, the wind blowing through my hair, and the wetness of the moss brushing my ankles distract me from the air hunger, the leg pain, and the developing blisters. My heart races in the last leg of the race as "runner's high" consumes me so that I have the energy to pass one more person before I cross the finish line. My breathing relapses, my muscles relax, and I look back to see all the runners I have passed . . . what an exhilarating moment!

Cross-country allows me to feel this great sense of accomplishment because of its focus on individual perseverance. Both intensive training and mental toughness are also equally important for success. There are times when running in practice that I find myself wondering why I push so hard. I think about stopping or even slowing down, but then I am over-whelmed by an inner voice that tells me to keep going. Listening to that voice, taking that extra challenge permits me to realize that had I slowed down or cut that last turn, I would have only been cheating myself.

Although cross-country is a highly individual sport, teamwork is nev-ertheless as important. Individuals score points for their respective teams during meets, which determines the overall performance of the team. Of twenty runners, only six of my teammates are girls; consequently, each member is critical because five runners are required to participate in a meet. It is also imperative that we encourage one another to gain the points necessary to win. I started on the team as a freshman, the under-dog. I did not know the running courses, I did not know how to pace myself, and I did not know how to use proper form. During that first sea-son alone, my running improved dramatically with the guidance and support of my coaches and teammates. Now I am a senior, and I have the privilege of helping the new freshmen. It is my job to help them find their way, to give them advice on their running style, or to say "good job" and pat them on their backs.

In a sport like cross-country, all one really needs is that pat on the back. The power that we all possess to motivate ourselves as well as others is one that is often hidden deep down inside, but once awakened, its effects are immeasurable. The end of the cross-country season will not mark the end of my motivation. Instead, I am now committed to go the extra mile in the race of life.

Georgetown University Essay

Please relate your interest in studying at Georgetown University to your fu-ture goals. How do these thoughts relate to your chosen course of study?

Mock Trial, Gap, Summer in Engineering . . . My involvement in a mul-titude of extracurricular activities, summer programs, and summer jobs and internships have exposed me to a myriad of career opportunities, yet I am still not certain of a definitive career. I plan to take the experiences I have acquired coming into Georgetown College and supplement them with the challenging academic curriculum offered by college. Together with my past experience and the education I will receive, I hope to find a perfect career match for me.

While Mock Trial and my internship at the office of Senator Paul Sar-banes gave me exposure to the fields of law and government, my job at the Gap and my internship at the Community Foundation of the Eastern Shore introduced me to business. I even had further hands-on experience with the business world when I founded and chaired my own Youth Foundation Fund. With the academic rigors as well as internship opportunities provided by Georgetown College, I can better understand the career fields that I am considering.

Exposure to stimulating students, challenging coursework, and motivating professors are what I hope to gain from attending Georgetown College. I am looking forward to being both academically and socially stimulated to achieve the best preparation and foundation possible for whatever career I may pursue in the future.

RECYCLING ESSAYS

I applied to eight colleges. At first, writing eight essays seemed overwhelming. With the headache of taking senior year AP level courses plus juggling many extracurricular activities, you want to minimize the time spent filling out applications as much as possible. With each college application requiring anywhere from one to three essays, you can spend forever writing. Instead, take a few minutes to organize ahead of time. Look at each of your applications and make a list of all of the essay topics that you will have to complete. Immediately, you will recognize that some of the essay topics will repeat and overlap. Essays asking you to write about a personal experience or to discuss an extracurricular activity are common themes that are more than likely to show up on more than one application. After doing this comparison, look to see how you can cut down on your list even further. For example, the University of Virginia asked the following question, and I accordingly wrote the following response:

If you could cause any one living person to change his or her mind about one thing, whom would you pick, and how would you change his or her thinking?

Yelping and squirming in my arms, my new puppy, Phoebe, tried to break through the glass of our car door, desperately calling out for her mother. Phoebe looked me in the eye and suddenly she seemed to quiet down. I stroked her soothingly as she curled up in my lap and nearly fell asleep. I cared for her with all my heart. My whole life, I had wanted nothing more than a dog. Every birthday wish was for a dog until finally, I had gotten my wish.

My mother had never owned a dog, let alone any other animal. She was terrified of them and even carried a stick when she went for walks in our neighborhood. The thought of getting our very own dog scared her even more; eventually, with much persuasion, she gave in. The agreement was that I would take care of Phoebe, including bathing, feeding, and walking her. But soon after we got her, I started my junior year of high school. Between schoolwork and after-school activities, I barely managed to make it home in time for dinner. The burden of taking care of Phoebe quickly fell on my mother.

After several weeks, situations changed. My mom became attached to Phoebe. We would sit on both sides of Phoebe, fussing over her and petting her until she finally fell asleep. My once timid mother was no longer afraid of animals.

So why did we have to give Phoebe away? My mother told me that although we all loved Phoebe, the truth was that she was a handful. I wanted more than anything to change her mind, and so I tried. I argued that Phoebe was one of the best things that had ever happened to us and that my mother especially needed her since I would be leaving the house soon. With two children away at school, she would need someone to keep her company. I also explained how Phoebe would provide protection. But most importantly, I pleaded that Phoebe was a part of our family and that she had shown us the meaning of unconditional love and loyalty.

There is not one day that goes by that my mother and I do not think about Phoebe. What is quite ironic is that I was successful in changing my mother's mind about animals, but I never did change her mind about owning one.

After writing this essay, I saw that Princeton asked another question that at first glance seemed quite different from the above question asked by the University of Virginia. But, with a few changes, I was able to use my UVA essay to answer the following question asked by Princeton:

Discuss something (anything) you just wished you understood better?
Yelping and squirming in my arms, my new puppy, Phoebe, tried to break through the glass of our car door, desperately calling out for her mother. Phoebe looked me in the eye and suddenly she seemed to quiet down. I stroked her soothingly as she curled up in my lap and nearly fell asleep. I cared for her with all my heart. My whole life, I had wanted nothing more than a dog. Every birthday wish was for a dog until finally, I had gotten my wish.

My mother had never owned a dog, let alone any other animal. She was terrified of them and even carried a stick when she went for walks in our neighborhood. The thought of getting our very own dog scared her even more; eventually, with much persuasion, she gave in. The agreement was that I would take care of Phoebe, including bathing, feeding, and walking her. But soon after we got her, I started my junior year of high school. Between schoolwork and after-school activities, I barely managed to make it home in time for dinner. The burden of taking care of Phoebe quickly fell on my mother.

After several weeks, situations changed. My mom became attached to her. We would sit on both sides of Phoebe, fussing over her and petting her until she would finally fall asleep. My once timid mother was no longer afraid of animals.

So why did we have to give Phoebe away? My mother told me that although we all loved Phoebe, the truth was that she was a handful. I wanted more than anything to change her mind, and so I tried. I argued that Phoebe was one of the best things that had ever happened to us and that my mother especially needed her since I would be leaving the house soon. With two children away at school, she would need someone to keep her company. I also explained how Phoebe would provide protection. But most importantly, I pleaded that Phoebe was a part of our family and that she had shown us the meaning of unconditional love and loyalty.

There is not one day that goes by that my mother and I do not think about Phoebe. Of course, she was a handful, but in my mind, the positives always outweighed any of her faults. What is ironic is that I was successful in changing my mother's mind about animals, but I never did change her mind about owning one. I wish I could understand why.

Another example of recycling essays is when Cornell asked me the following: "'A stone, a leaf, an unfound door.' *Look Homeward, Angel,* Thomas Wolfe. Write about three objects that would give the admissions selection committee insight into who you are." After already writing essays on an extracurricular activity (cross-country) and on a personal experience (Girl Scouts) for other applications, at first glance I thought I was going to have to write an entirely new essay. But with a little tweaking and a little advance planning, I instead only had to do a little cutting and pasting. For one of my objects, I picked sneakers; I could then incorporate my cross-country essay. I also picked a switch plate, so I could then insert parts of my Girl Scouts essay. This daunting essay was already two-thirds complete before I even started.

A switch plate, smelly sneakers, and a soft, cuddly stuffed beaver (MIT's mascot) . . . these three things may ordinarily contain no special meaning to a person. However, each of these objects represents a different side of me, making them some of my most prized possessions.

I recently completed my Girl Scout Gold Award project, the highest award a Girl Scout can achieve. To earn this award, I sold my hand-painted switch plates and used the money generated from their sales to purchase food supplies. I then coordinated a group of students, either from high school or from my local temple, to make peanut butter and jelly sandwiches to donate to a local shelter. This project brought community awareness, especially to my temple, where community service projects were rarely carried out. From "Daisies to Seniors," Girl Scouts has been an important part of my life, showing me the importance of contributing to my community.

Not only does my switch plate represent an important facet of my life, but my smelly sneakers do as well. Running varsity cross-country has allowed me to feel a great sense of accomplishment because of its focus on individual perseverance. Both intensive training and mental toughness are equally important for success. There are times when practicing that I find myself wondering why I push so hard. I think about stopping or even slowing down, but then I am overwhelmed by an inner voice that tells me to keep going.

Listening to that voice, taking that extra challenge permits me to realize that had I slowed down or cut that last turn, I would have only been cheating myself. Cross-country is not one of the most popular sports, but for me it is one of the most rewarding.

One of the most essential parts of my life has always been my family, and my stuffed beaver is the gift my brother sent me on my birthday during his first year away at college. When I was younger, it seemed I was never far behind my older brother, Vinay. Vinay's favorite color was yellow, so mine was also. His lucky number was eight and that became mine as well. As the years went on, I grew my own identity, but I never stopped looking up to him. To me, he is the epitome of a perfect brother. He would always look after me or save me that last piece of cake in the refrigerator. These may seem like trivial incidents, but these were the actions that touched my heart the most. Vinay left for MIT more than three years ago. He had been only a door away from me for the past fourteen years and now he would be hundreds of miles away in Boston. However, I was wrong in thinking we would stop being in touch. Our relationship seemed to grow even closer when he left. We are now seniors preparing for completely different futures. He is applying to medical schools; I am applying to colleges. The decisions we make may cause us to be even further apart than Salisbury is from Boston, but the bond that we share will keep us close, forever.

My switch plate, my smelly sneakers, and my stuffed animal each tell a different story about my life. They hold special meaning and each part contributes in creating my identity.

TWELVE

Recommendation Letters

"In a pool of thousands of applicants—most of whom have impressive grades, relatively high standardized test scores and substantial involvement in extracurricular activities—How do you separate yourself from the pack? A great recommendation can make all the difference" (Krouse, 56). Most parents and students do not know that the recommendation letter is one of the most crucial factors within the college admissions process because through it colleges see the applicant behind the grades and test scores. Our experiences taught us not to ignore any of the aspects of this involved procedure.

When my son went through the admissions process, we did not consider recommendation letters as an important factor in his plans. He personally handed all of these recommendation letters to his teachers, and we let the process take its own course. We did not learn that a teacher recommendation letter was missing until a college rejection letter arrived.

In addition, we later found out that certain teachers were not good writers. Even though they strongly endorsed my son's work and character, they were not able to articulate their support in a convincing manner in order to make it an outstanding recommendation. In a highly selective college, a strong recommendation letter can add to your application and help it stand out from the pool. We realized that not only is it important that the teacher think highly of the applicant, but it is also crucial that he or she be a good, descriptive writer who can give a clear portrait of the student. No matter how much a teacher may like you, the effect of a recommendation can be weakened when poorly written.

With this experience, we became more cautious in our approach to teacher recommendations. We realized that we had to take responsibility into our own hands and become proactive. When my daughter went through this process, she made sure that the recommendation reached the institution before the application deadline by taking a few precautionary steps.

Sheila gave teachers an addressed and stamped envelope indicating

105

"teacher recommendation" when initially handing out the recommendation forms and descriptions. She then asked the teachers to place their
completed recommendation letters in the envelope and give it to the guidance counselor, who mailed all parts of the application together *or* had
the teachers themselves mail the form directly to the college. She then followed up by calling the college two weeks after she'd mailed her application to make sure the recommendation letters had been received. (Keep
in mind that because the colleges are swamped with applications, there
may be a lapse of days or weeks from when the college receives your application until the time that they have it registered on the computer.) Once
she received confirmation that the college had received the recommendation letter, she made special note of it in her journal or planner.

You should also realize that each college refers to their recommendation forms differently. For example, they may name it as Form A/Form
B, Teacher 1/Teacher 2, or Teacher A/ Teacher B. In other words, if you
apply to eight colleges, you will have sixteen teacher recommendations
that will need to be completed by various teachers. So in order to avoid
confusion and to keep track of all of the different college recommendation
forms and the names of the corresponding teacher to which these forms
had been submitted, Sheila made a chart, on which she recorded the following:

1. All of the different recommendation form numbers from each college
2. The names of the teachers filling out each corresponding college
   form, matching each form, A or B, with a particular teacher
3. The dates that the recommendation forms were submitted
4. The application deadline for each form
5. The dates of when the forms were mailed to the colleges

Each teacher receives numerous recommendation requests from several
different students, and most students give their evaluation letters to the
same favorite teachers. The chances of one of these forms being misplaced
are quite likely. If you are organized enough to record all of this information on a chart, the process will help you to keep track of what is missing
and to make the inevitable more manageable. All you have to do is to
refer to your chart to trace the missing form and find out the corresponding college, then call that particular college and get another application.
This way you can avoid a lot of chaos and confusion during your application process.

Sheila also gave the teachers enough notice (notifying them as early as
the summer after her junior year), to let them know that she was consider-

ing asking them for a teacher recommendation in the fall. This way the teacher had plenty of time to make detailed notes, if needed.

A COMPLETE LISTING OF RECOMMENDATION LETTER CONSIDERATIONS

Basic Requirements

In our experience, most selective colleges needed the following recommendations:

1. Two teacher recommendation letters
2. One recommendation from either the guidance counselor or the high school principal
3. References from a sports coach or from work, if requested

Choosing Your Teachers

These recommendation letters play an important role in your admissions process. A strong recommendation can increase your chances of acceptance. Start thinking as early as your junior or even your sophomore year as to which teachers you would choose to write your recommendation letters. Get to know them well. Always treat your teachers with respect.

1. Go to teachers who know you well. Ask preferably those who have had you in classes for one or two years. Especially ask teachers with whom you are taking classes in your junior and senior year, as they can identify you as a developed student and worker. According to *An Introduction to Harvard College*, "Teachers who know the applicant well and who have taught him or her in academic subjects (preferably in the final two years of secondary school) most often provide us the most valuable testimony" (47).
2. Choose teachers in whose class you did your best.
3. Choose teachers who will be able to add favorably to your profile. They should write honestly, emphasizing your strengths while also explaining your weaknesses. You may even ask the teacher if he or she would be able to give you a stellar recommendation. From their responses you will get some sort of an idea as to how they feel about you.
4. Choose teachers who write well. Talk to some senior students or your guidance counselor and get feedback as to which teachers write good recommendation letters.

5. Most applications will have instructions as to which teachers should fill out their recommendation forms. Many selective colleges need two teachers' recommendations: one from an English or foreign language teacher and one from a math or science teacher. If the teacher's subject is not specified, then you may choose a teacher whose subject area is something you would like to pursue as a major in college.

6. Choose teachers who are dependable, reliable, and who will mail your recommendations promptly. A simple thing such as a letter of recommendation not being sent on time can jeopardize your application.

7. It is to your advantage if the teacher who writes your recommendation letter also knows you outside the classroom. For example, Sheila asked her chemistry teacher, also an assistant coach for the cross-country team, for a letter of recommendation. This way your recommendation can be more than one-dimensional. Sheila's teacher was able to not only identify her academic perseverance but also to describe her as a determined person based on how he saw her on the sports field.

8. In a recent interview with Dean Fitzsimmons, dean of undergraduate admissions at Harvard College, he stated: "In a recommendation letter, we generally look for three areas of commentary: academic, extracurricular, and personal qualities. Extracurricular includes both school activities and other outside commitments such as home duties, work responsibilities, and community involvement. In terms of the assessment of personal qualities, we look for people who are going to be interesting as roommates and who are described as active in the classroom and extracurricular activities. We are also looking for evidence that demonstrates who this person will become in say twenty-five or fifty years. For example, say that a student has a SAT II score of 760, a 5 on AP, and A's in class. This is fine, but in the letter of recommendation we are looking for more of the intangibles. We look for students who have an unusual academic curiosity and a love of ideas, but we are not hoping to find 'grade grubbers' who grimly go through their academic work without much creativity or enthusiasm."

Therefore, make sure you select a teacher who can thoroughly explain your personal qualities and with whom you share mutual respect.

Outside Recommendations

You may sometimes require recommendation letters from people other than teachers and guidance counselors. In choosing a person, you want to think about the same things as you would when choosing a teacher, such as someone who knows you well and who could present you in the best light. You may consider asking a coach or an employer. But heed the advice of Dean Fitzsimmons, dean of undergraduate admissions at Harvard, when he writes: "Outside recommendations can often be very helpful. One received outside recommendation was from the custodian of the school who supervised the prospective student's work program. This recommendation provided real insight into the student's personality and was more helpful than a letter from a famous person or an alumnus who does not even know the student. It is also important to keep in mind that too many recommendations can detract from a student's profile."

Letter Etiquette

Write a formal letter to your teacher requesting his or her recommendation. Teachers need more than a casual between-class conversation in order to remember your recommendation letter request.

Supplying a Résumé

Hand teachers your résumé and highlight information you would like them to mention. This reminds them of a student's achievements in and outside of the classroom; information that is mentioned in your evaluation can reinforce what is on your application.

Suggesting an Anecdote

You may give a letter to your teacher that includes specific anecdotes that you would like him or her to mention in the recommendation. Cite significant contributions, such as when you took trigonometry in eleventh grade or that you also helped her to correct papers for her ninth grade class. These notes not only show a teacher's confidence in your ability, but they also make the recommendation more meaningful and powerful.

Making an Informal Request

As mentioned before, you may jump-start the process by informally indicating to the teachers as early as possible that you would like a letter of recommendation. I (Sheila) strongly recommend writing teachers letters at the end of your junior year, noting that you will be asking them for a recommendation in the fall. With the letter, I would also supply a résumé. This way you will give them plenty of notice, and some teachers may take advantage of the time to begin to write your recommendation letter in the summer. They will have extra time to be detailed and thorough with your recommendation, and this care also reflects positively on your organizational skills and ability to plan ahead.

You also may request of teachers to write your evaluation letters while you are attending their class. This way they can note any of your unique qualities, such as how you stimulated the class discussions, while it is still fresh in their minds. They might have forgotten these contributions when they write your recommendation a year or two later. They may even be able to cite your significant contributions, such as how you stayed after school to tutor other students. Not only does this demonstrate the teacher's confidence in you, it also makes the recommendation more noteworthy and powerful. Request them to keep the letter in your school file and refer to it later when needed.

Using Courtesy

If you find you need a teacher for a recommendation letter in your senior year, try to give it to him or her at least a month before the application deadline. Remember that each student may apply from anywhere to one to ten different colleges and will request his or her evaluations from the same teacher. Writing recommendations for several students takes a lot of a teachers' time, especially within a large public school. Thus, the sooner you make your request, the more likely you will meet the application deadline. Because teachers will be receiving a plethora of requests, be courteous when asking them. Make sure to ask *early*!

Waiving Your Rights

You have two options: to waive your rights to see the letters of recommendation or not to. It is strongly suggested that you do waive your rights, meaning that the letter is confidential and you have not read it. When you waive your rights, colleges consider the recommendations more seriously. Using this method, the teacher can write freely and colleges therefore view these recommendation letters as more honest appraisals than ones that the students have read. Sign the waiver before you submit your recommendation form to the teacher.

Giving Requests to Teachers

1. Before you give the teacher the recommendation, be sure to fill out your personal information, such as name and address, that the form requests.
2. Include the application deadline dates in your teachers' references.

3. Provide your teachers with instructions as to what to do with the letter.

4. Attach a preaddressed, stamped envelope to the recommendation form so that the teacher can mail it directly to the college, or instruct the teacher to give a sealed recommendation letter to the guidance counselor, who can mail your entire application in one packet. This way you can be sure that the teacher recommendation was sent. Further, it will allow you to present an organized, neat application packet to the college. The college will receive all parts of the application at the same time and can start processing it as soon as possible. This is especially crucial for schools with rolling admissions.

Labeling the Information

We found it useful to type the addresses on labels and stick them onto the envelope. We typed the contents of the packet onto a second, larger label, which was placed on the lower left hand corner of the envelope. Teachers are swamped with requests for recommendations. Adding an address label makes it is one less thing for the teacher to do and helps to keep him or her organized.

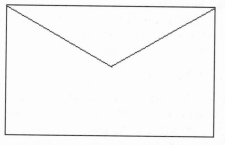

Do *not* put anything in bulky folders. This is a nuisance for admissions officers!

Write a Thank-You Note

Send thank-you notes to your teachers promptly, or at least two weeks before the application deadline. Sending a thank-you note to the appropriate teacher before the application deadline can serve as a polite reminder for him or her to complete the letter if he or she has not yet done so.

Writing the Actual Letter

The following is useful information for teachers, administration, and parents.

1. A common mistake is that teachers do not usually highlight the student's academic performance in the classroom. Instead, they are tempted to concentrate on grades and GPA, thinking that they speak for the student's academic potential. However, colleges are not interested in these areas alone. They can see grades on the student's transcript. Instead, they want to know information such as the student's passion for learning, involvement and participation in the classroom, initiative, and preparedness for class. This description will provide admissions officers with key information that a transcript alone will fail to tell. "The key word . . . is initiative because this is the most important characteristic we select for. We try to admit people who take initiative in their lives, who take responsibility for their education. Many students study hard, get good grades and good scores. But many of those do it because it is a family expectation or community pressure or a myriad of other reasons" (Tse, 6).
2. Highly selective colleges are looking for movers and shakers, individuals who will be an asset to the school and enrich the student body.
3. As noted in *An Introduction to Harvard College*, "Comprehensive reports from your teachers in two different academic subjects further clarify your academic and personal profile" (39).
4. Teachers frequently do not stress enough the student's academic potential. Instead, they concentrate on their personal qualities and their final grades. Teachers' recommendations with appropriate information can enhance the student's academic profile. If the student wishes to be an English major, a detailed recommendation from an English teacher emphasizing his or her passion and strong improvement in the subject is far more telling than an enumeration of the grades received.
5. It is also useful in a teacher's recommendation letter to compare a student's academic achievement and potential to the other members of the class.
6. Adjectives such as "painstaking" used in the letter may be judged as unfavorable to the student's image and may make him or her seem programmed, perhaps even boring. Michele A. Hernández, formerly Dartmouth's admissions officer, comments on how admissions officers may interpret the connotations of "diligent and conscientious." She writes, "Admission officers at highly selective colleges tend to

interpret words like these to mean that the student is merely a hard worker, or a grind but not a very insightful or naturally bright student. Diligent implies that a student dutifully plows through assignment after assignment without ever reaching any deep insight or adding to the class in any way." She also mentions that several students were rejected because they came across as merely diligent, lacking that extra spark that sets them apart from the rest of the class (Hernández, 140).

7. Teachers should try to mention how many A's were given out in the class (if it is a difficult level class). For example, a student might have had B's in a class where the class average was a C. As Marilee Jones, dean of MIT admissions, notes, "The admissions officers take everything into consideration. For example, there are applicants from high schools of different calibers. When we begin to make decisions, we know that in some schools, B's are perfectly acceptable" (Tse, 6). Make grade charts that note the number of students versus grade distribution. Given this information, the officer can get an insightful picture of the applicants themselves, the difficulty of the courses, the demands of teachers, and the overall comparisons of the applicant with his or her peers.

8. Statements such as "he made other students look like children" are profound and show the admissions officers the respect that the teacher has for the student and the student's level of maturity as compared to his or her peers.

Avoiding Problems

Avoid having celebrities or elected officials write letters for you if you do not have a profound relationship with them. However, if you interned in the office of the mayor, then a strong letter would be quite powerful and advantageous.

THIRTEEN

The Guidance Counselor

Your high school guidance counselor has a key role in the college application process. Almost all selective colleges have an evaluation or recommendation form to be completed by the guidance counselor or school principal. Your guidance counselor is the only person who has the opportunity to provide a comprehensive letter that highlights your progress throughout all four years of high school.

Guidance counselors advise students as to which courses to take in high school and help plan extracurricular activities as early as freshman year. They can even suggest for each student which teachers would provide the best recommendations. Counselors have usually worked with teachers over many years and have an idea about which teachers write detailed and personalized letters of recommendation in contrast with those who tend to write generic letters. They also know which teachers write their letters promptly, versus those who may not send their letters on time.

In public schools, guidance counselors usually want to offer academic counseling but are often overworked with addressing the students' social issues. Thus, their efforts to offer academic advice can be very limited. That is why it is very crucial that parents and students take an active role in the college application process to supplement the counselor's work. In order to assist the counselor, students should try to establish a healthy relationship with him or her starting from the first year of high school.

Your approach to the guidance counselor should be polite yet persistent because guidance counselors may forget about certain application deadlines. Guidance counselors will receive a plethora of recommendation requests. It is to your advantage to give them plenty of notice; at least one month before the application deadline should be appropriate. Visiting the counselor once per week in advance of a deadline may be necessary to avoid a potentially disastrous situation where an application is not read because it was not received on time. In order to reduce your counselor's work, fill in your personal information on the evaluation form before you give it to your counselor. Make sure to fill in your name, address, social security number, your senior year courses, and any other requested information.

Guidance counselors are usually asked to provide a comprehensive report based on your achievements and developments throughout all four years of high school. Make sure you submit upfront all the pertinent information that your guidance counselor would need, including a résumé, grade report, and any specific forms that he or she may need to fill out. With this information available, the counselor is able to write an effective and persuasive recommendation/evaluation. A guidance counselor's report can provide an in-depth recommendation that highlights your strengths and tactfully explains your weaknesses. This evaluation becomes especially important in special circumstances, such as a drop in grades due to a family tragedy. The recommendation can also reinforce what is on your application, such as an outstanding accomplishment in or out of the classroom.

High school guidance counselors provide information that explains your school's grading system and curriculum. This includes answers to the following:

1. Are the grades weighted or unweighted?
2. What is the corresponding GPA in each scenario?
3. What is the student's class ranking, and how many students are involved in this system?
4. What is the level of difficulty of the applicant's course load? This evaluation can be classified as less demanding than average, average, more demanding than average, or most demanding.

Competitive colleges select students who maintain a high GPA, obtain a high class ranking, and who take the most challenging classes. All of this information will be in your transcript written by your guidance counselor.

Guidance counselors should also include a school profile showing the admissions officers what percentage of students go to a four-year college, what opportunities were available to you, and how well you took advantage of what was offered. An example would be if your school offers ten AP courses and you took none as opposed to taking the most challenging classes that were available to you. They will look to see if you took all easy courses to maintain a high GPA or if you actually took harder classes. A school profile is also extremely important for those students who apply to colleges that may not be familiar with their high school.

IMPORTANT POINTS TO REMEMBER

1. Guidance counselors have to fill out a personal profile.
2. Give your counselor a stamped envelope, preaddressed to the colleges to which you are applying.
3. Guidance counselors can also gather all parts of your application and mail it for you. This includes sending the following elements:
   - A sealed and signed teacher's recommendation
   - Your application
   - Transcript and guidance counselor evaluation form
   - A check for the application fees (or a waiver, if appropriate)

   Remember to indicate on the outside of the envelope which forms are enclosed. Below is a sample of the way I presented all the parts of the application to the colleges to which I applied. I created labels for each individual form such as teacher recommendation, guidance counselor evaluation form, my part of the application, and so on, and then placed these separate forms into their own envelopes. Finally, I placed all of these envelopes in one large envelope with its contents displayed (using labels) on the front as shown below:

College X
Name
Enclosed Within: Social Security #
✓Application
✓School Report
✓Teacher Recommendation

4. Write a prompt thank-you note to your guidance counselor, thanking him or her for the effort and time put into your application.
5. Record when the guidance counselor report was mailed and when it was received by the college.

6. Guidance counselors must follow up your progress by submitting a midterm report to update the admissions office about your first semester's grades. Keep track of the deadline dates for submitting the midterm reports to various colleges. Give your guidance counselor enough notice to complete these forms.

FOURTEEN

Hiring an Independent Counselor

DO YOU NEED AN INDEPENDENT COUNSELOR?

In today's competitive college admissions process, consulting an independent counselor has become increasingly popular. However, private counselors are costly. They may charge anywhere from $2,000 to $2,500, a flat fee for four years, and work with your child throughout his or her high school years at different stages of the admissions process. Some counselors may offer their services for an hourly rate of anywhere from $100 to $150. These figures are an approximate estimation and subject to change, but they should give you an idea of the independent counselors' fees. With these rates, hiring an independent counselor has its disadvantages. But there are other advantages to consider.

In some large public schools, the number of students assigned to a guidance counselor can be overwhelming. For example, at our high school there were three guidance counselors for approximately 1,100 to 1,200 students. In addition, school counselors must deal with class scheduling and social issues such as drugs, violence, and teenage pregnancy. Thus, their efforts to help the students are diffused. Your school counselor might also be new and inexperienced when it comes to assisting students with the college admissions process. Counselors want to help but do not have time to provide the specific guidance and assistance that each student may require during his or her college admissions process. Thus, responsibility falls on parents and the students to take an active role. However, if you can afford the costs of the independent counselor, you may want to consider hiring one. It is your choice.

Parents and students should keep in mind that the fall of the senior year is a very busy time. As seniors, students not only have to fill out college applications but also have to keep up with their test grades, schoolwork, sports practice, school dances, football games, extracurricular activities, and jobs. Some may even be taking their standardized tests in SAT II or I in the fall of their senior year. Because of this pressure, students may tend to procrastinate with their admissions process work. Unlike school guidance counselors, independent counselors are not affiliated with your high school. They work independently throughout the applicant's high school career, even starting as early as the freshman year. This type of guidance may assist the worried parent and student. However, many admissions officers do not look favorably on the use of an independent counselor. Admissions officers could perceive this assistance as students being programmed by the counselor. So if you plan to hire an independent counselor, it would be wise to be discreet about it.

If you do hire a counselor to aid in this process, do not expect him or her to work miracles. On the other hand, counselors can be helpful with things such as helping you develop your essay response so that it is appropriate for you. In addition, good independent counselors can guide and assist students in arranging their profile and chronologically organizing their extracurricular activities such as sports, volunteer work, leadership roles, job experience, and student government. They can assist with the fine-tuning of details such as making the number of hours and the number of weeks that a student committed to a particular activity more presentable or recording all of the student's activities, which he or she may perceive as too insignificant; however, such activities can enhance his or her application. Independent counselors will also remind clients to document all of the activities they were involved in that they might have forgotten when they quickly filled out their applications.

Counselors can also give you a realistic assessment about which colleges to apply to. This recommendation is based on different factors such as test scores, grades, extracurricular activities, and prospective major. They can advise you as to which schools might be your safety schools, which ones would be within-reach schools, and those that are definitely far-reach schools.

With all that they can do, counselors should not write your application essay. They can, however, give you feedback as to if your message is clear and your true personality is portrayed. They can also help you with the selection of your topic. If you are very passionate about a certain activity or commitment and want to brag about it in your essay, they can make sure that you brag about your accomplishments *politely.*

FACTORS TO CONSIDER WHEN PICKING AN INDEPENDENT COUNSELOR

1. Location. How far do you have to travel? You may have to set several appointments with your independent counselor, some of which may be on a school night, so make sure the driving distance

round trip is appropriate for you. Would you be comfortable with a one-hour or two-hour drive one way? Sometimes you do not have much of a choice since there may not be any counselors within your desired reach.

2. Cost. Are the fees hourly based or flat rate? Some independent counselors may work with an hourly rate of $100 to $200. Others may charge a flat rate for four years, which is paid in installments. These fees may vary anywhere from $2,000 to $3,000.

3. What are the special services rendered? The range of services offered by different counselors includes helping students strategically plan their academic course selection and extracurricular counseling. Counselors can advise on standardized testing, suggest useful résumé-enhancing summer activities, and provide tips on the application process, writing the college essay, and the interview. Check with the independent counselors for the specific services they offer since these may vary from one to another.

ADVANTAGES OF AN INDEPENDENT COUNSELOR

Independent counselors offer the same kind of guidance the best high schools and prestigious private schools can offer.

1. They can help students evaluate their priorities.
2. They can offer advice for planning academic activities in the student's freshman year.
3. They can offer planning for extracurricular activities in the freshman year.
4. They can help students organize all of their activities in their senior year.
5. They will suggest that students make a list of their career goals that can help them to think about their future plans.
6. They can schedule students' required completions of the SAT I and SAT II, suggesting which date, month, and year students should take these tests.
7. They can customize and narrow the list of applicable colleges.

CONCLUSION

To summarize, independent counselors can offer you, as any good high school counselor can, advice concerning the admissions process. They can also assist you in organizing and presenting your application, thus helping to market a student's college application by highlighting talents and achievements that are not reflected in academic records. While many students believe that they do not need a private consultant's advice, there may be others that do. Some students may have access to all the resources, advice, and guidance that is needed for the college application process available to them at their school, while other students, due to lack of school funding, may find it difficult to get the same degree of service at their schools.

Because all of these resources and the necessary information for college applications are available, parents and students can do some research on their own and save a lot of money. However, if you decide to hire a consultant, make sure your money is well spent. Find out the number of colleges that the individual has recently visited. Check his or her credibility and track record whenever possible by asking for résumés and references. Once again, it is your choice.

To find a list of counselors near you, write to:

The Independent Educational Consultant Association
P.O. Box 125
Forestdale, MA 02644

FIFTEEN

The Wait List

NINE USEFUL TIPS IF YOU ARE WAIT LISTED

1. If placed on a wait list at a certain college, you have to decide whether you are still interested in attending that particular college, if admitted.
2. However, each college has different wait list policies. Call the particular college for which you are wait listed and inquire about their wait list procedure.
3. Find out how many students are wait listed and the percentage of students that were admitted from their wait list in the previous years.
4. If you are wait listed, colleges usually mail a postcard on which you are to indicate whether you are still interested in admission to that college. You should promptly mail your reply if you are still interested in the school.
5. Write a letter restating your interest in that college.
6. Ask the school counselor to call the college to emphasize your interest and to inquire about your chances for admission. He or she should request a list of materials that are still needed in order to update your application file.
7. Send any updated information, such as your latest transcript grades, sports awards, scholarships, new activities, or any significant accomplishment that is not mentioned in the original application.
8. Call and talk to the admissions officer. (Request to speak preferably to a regional officer from your area.)
9. If you had a good campus interview with admissions personnel, you may contact him or her for assistance.

STUDENTS' EXPERIENCES

Here are some experiences of past students facing the wait list and how they handled it. We are not sure if these students eventually received admission to the colleges because of these tactics or because of something else, but nevertheless we found them quite interesting.

Jane's Story

Sometimes a sensitive letter written by a mother or sibling to an admissions officer vouching and testifying in favor of their daughter/sister can help. Jane did not receive admission to Harvard when she first applied. She was instead placed on the wait list. In early summer, she was offered a chance to defer one year and be granted admission for the following year. Jane chose not to take this option but to chance the wait list. Without her knowledge, her sisters and her brother wrote letters from the heart explaining why they thought their sister should be admitted. Her brother explained how Jane was always there to tutor him and made the extra effort to help him with his studies. Her sisters explained how Jane was instrumental in helping the family, especially since their mother was raising them by herself. Maybe the admissions officers found the letters very touching. At any rate, Jane was admitted to Harvard for the upcoming year.

John's Story

First of all, when John was wait listed, he mailed the postcard promptly to indicate that he was still interested in that college. Then he made sure to send a deposit to his second-choice college, to which he had been accepted. He persuaded his guidance counselor to call the first-choice college. He sent new information that had not been included on his original application, such as his receipt of many scholarships and awards through May of his senior year, to the college. It was very important to update his files with credentials that would favorably add to his application, yet he was cautious not to aggravate the admissions officer with superfluous information.

He made a visit to the college, where he took a tour and stopped by the admissions office. All of this determination paid off, as he did get admitted. He later found out that eight hundred applicants were wait listed and only eighteen were eventually accepted.

Jane and John's stories show that unorthodox methods sometimes pay off, making your application stand out from the wait list pool. However, the student takes a lot of risk with these excessive procedures. In some cases risk taking can pay off, while in others it can hurt, especially if it does not portray your true self.

SIXTEEN

Time Management

[Vinay wrote this entire chapter based on his four years of experience at MIT.]

Time management is one of the most important skills that students must learn in order to be successful in college. Mastery of this skill will reflect an ability to handle many tasks at once without compromising individual effort in any one area. Many employers carefully examine a student's academic experiences for evidence of this ability. Unfortunately, time management is tough to teach and can only be learned by trial and error.

The transition from high school to college is a significant one. Students face the transition from high school, where every activity is structured and organized, to college, where young adults are forced to make their own schedules with virtually no adult assistance or supervision. During the first year of college, students want to participate in all types of clubs and events. However, because they are not familiar with the time demands of a college curriculum and each type of extracurricular activity, students generally have a tough time correlating their activities and class schedules during the first semester. Sometimes students suffer the most stress when dealing with the effects of an overcrowded schedule. Students who spend too much time with extracurricular activities usually do not spend enough time with their schoolwork, which can severely affect their course grades. During my freshman year, many of my friends were playing varsity sports, rushing a fraternity, and joining extracurricular clubs. Not realizing the demanding requirements for these activities, my friends found that they were not spending enough time studying and were struggling to pass their classes.

However, it is possible to participate in activities and still get good grades. In fact, four years later when you are applying for jobs or graduate schools, most employers expect applicants to have a decent GPA and to have participated in several extracurricular activities. In time, my friends realized the time commitments of each activity and were able to participate in all the activities they were interested in without sacrificing their grades. Moreover, one should be encouraged to participate in extracurricular activities. Harvard's motto, for example, is that "you learn just as much outside the classroom as you do inside the classroom." This philosophy applies to any college. Students grow just as much through their involvement in campus activities and their meetings with other students outside of the classroom as they do in the classroom. College students who go through college with very few activities or those who do not have good grades are sometimes seen as weaker candidates who lack good time management skills. When we then consider this necessary balance of study and participation, how does a student improve his or her time management skills? This chapter has several tips that will help you develop your own techniques to succeed in college.

1. Use a calendar. I have found it extremely useful to buy a planner at the beginning of the school year and write down all of my test dates and due dates for papers and projects. These deadlines are usually given to the students on the first day of class as part of the syllabus for the semester. Instructors generally adhere to this plan, so you can adequately plot your semester for all classes at the beginning of the term. Being aware of important test dates allows you to plan ahead and minimizes the need for last minute cramming. If you have a large project for a class, break it up into smaller, manageable sections. For a research paper, I would typically set four different dates with different milestones to complete by each date. The first milestone would be to complete the research and the second would be to make a rough outline of the paper. Thirdly, I would choose a date for the completion of the rough draft for the paper. This usually included making a few trips to the school's writing center to have another person evaluate the draft and provide constructive criticism for my revision process. The fourth and final milestone I noted was to finalize the paper by proofreading it and making a title page and a full bibliography.

2. Limit the amount of time allotted for playing video games and watching TV. Too often, I have found a friend or myself wasting time watching TV or playing video games. While it is okay to participate in either activity, they both tend to take up more time than one would expect. Many people say that they will play a video game for only one hour, but then they get so engrossed in the game that they end up spending much more time than that because of the game's alluring appeal. The same holds true for television. If you really want to watch a show or play a game, make a deal with yourself that you will stop after a certain amount of time, no matter how lazy you

feel. If you do not think that you will have the will power to stop, ask one of your friends to knock on your door or have someone go to the library with you at a certain time. Students are more likely to stop watching TV or playing games when they make a prior commitment to study with someone else. If you have a VCR, you can record your favorite show and watch it when you come back from the library. That way you have finished studying and you will not feel guilty about watching TV. The show will serve as a reward for completed studies. I avoided buying a TV and put off buying a computer so that I would minimize the distractions in my room.

3. Use your spare time for something productive. When in school, I would often come back to my room from class with the intention of studying for a few hours before our dinnertime. However, most of the time I would sit around and hang out with people until dinner, not accomplishing any of my goals. Sure, there are days when you just want to go back to your room and relax. But if you want to be productive, go to the library or a quiet place away from your room for an hour and study the lecture that you just finished in your schedule. This tactic was extremely useful because the material was fresh in my mind and it took me less time to learn the material than it would have if I had waited several days to review it. If you evaluate your day, you will realize that there are many times of the day where you are free for ten minutes, sometimes even up to an hour. Plan on using that time for something productive, like reviewing your lecture notes or making a schedule for the rest of the day. Whenever I did laundry, I would try to read through a lecture during those two hours rather than sitting around and doing nothing.

4. Make a schedule that is reasonable. I was most productive when I made a schedule for the evening and stuck to it. I also learned to make sure that I created a schedule that I could follow with accuracy. I usually started by making a to-do list and then built a schedule around all the tasks that I needed to accomplish by the end of the night. To perfect the schedule's accuracy and effectiveness, while you are doing certain activities, take a note of how long it takes to complete each task. Do not schedule only ten minutes for dinner when it may really take you a half an hour to eat and socialize. Also, do not underestimate the amount of time that it will take for you to learn a certain lecture or to compose an essay. You will be constantly off schedule if you budget a half an hour to learn a subject when you normally take two hours. This also applies to those who tend to overestimate the length of an activity. Some of my friends would set very low goals for themselves, so when they finished reading a lecture in two hours instead of four, they felt that they had already ac-

complished the day's goals and could relax for the rest of the night. Students who consistently do this may realize at the end of the semester that there is material that they did not have time to review, so they are forced into cramming for a subject. There is no benefit to making a schedule that you do not follow; it is equivalent to not making a schedule at all.

5. Learn to diagnose and to avoid signs of procrastination. Some people cannot concentrate while they are studying and will find any excuse for procrastination. The best way to avoid procrastination is to be aware of what is distracting you. Are you having trouble studying because you want to know the score of a game? Are you dying to talk to your friends to see how their day went? Whatever the reason for procrastinating, I found it helpful to take planned breaks in order to minimize the distractions while I was studying. I would work for fifty minutes consecutively and then take a ten-minute break to do whatever it was that would have normally lured me away from studying. By taking a planned break, you are allowing yourself to focus on your work for an extended period of time without many distractions. This strategy allows people to be more efficient and often finish their task in a shorter amount of time because they are not procrastinating.

6. Always avoid the all-nighter. If you make a schedule and stick to it, you should not have to stay up all night before a big exam. Some people can pull all-nighters, but most people cannot. People stay up all night before a big exam because they have not covered all the material and are forced to cram the information before the test. If you follow all of the previous suggestions, this will not be an issue because you will not need to cram the night before an exam. Make sure you get plenty of sleep two nights before a test and get decent sleep the night before the test. With enough rest and preparation, you should be able to cruise through any exam.

APPENDIX

College Supply List

Electronic Supplies/Accessories

1. Desk lamp, light bulbs
2. Fan
3. Computers/laptop
4. Modem
5. Printer, paper
6. Computer disks
7. Phone, answering machine
8. CD/tape recorder, CDs and tapes
9. Clock radio
10. Extension cord and power strip with surge protector
11. TV/ TV stand
12. VCR player
13. Camera, films
14. Iron, ironing board
15. Small broom or vacuum cleaner.

School Stationery
1. Pens, holder
2. Pencils/mechanical pencils
3. Paper clips
4. Rubber bands
5. Scotch tape
6. Staples
7. Scissors
8. College-ruled Paper, folders
9. Note pads, stick-on notes
10. Eraser, white out
11. Ruler
12. Dictionary

13. Thesaurus
14. Backpack
15. Weekly planner/pocket calendar
16. Envelopes and stamps

Personal/Dorm Supplies
1. Cash, including quarters for laundry
2. Registration information
3. Tuitions fees statement
4. College admission papers
5. Housing confirmation papers
6. College course catalog, your class schedule
7. Bank account, checkbook
8. Credit card/debit card
9. Social security card
10. Driver's license
11. Health insurance card
12. Sleeping bag
13. Blanket/comforter
14. Bed sheet sets
15. Pillow
16. Hangers
17. Memo board
18. Stick-on hooks
19. Posters
20. Pictures, photo album
21. Phone/address/ e-mail address
22. High school yearbook
23. Umbrella
24. Toiletries/bath supplies
25. Medicine/first aid kit
26. Sewing kit
27. Bath towels, beach towel
28. Sports equipment, water bottle, hobby supply
29. Crates
30. Rug
31. Wastebasket
32. Tissue box
33. Toolbox
34. Personal clothes: casual/formal/workout
35. Caps, jackets, gloves
36. Shoes: sneakers, formal, flip flops
37. Sunglasses

38. Cup, plate, spoons, etc.
39. Detergent
40. Nail cutter
41. Toothpaste and brush
42. Lotion, cologne, sun block

WORKS CITED

ACT, Inc. "General Questions on the ACT Assessment." At www.act.org/aap/ faq/general.html (accessed October 15, 2001).

Binswanger, C. K. "Check 'Em Out: 99 Top Websites." *Kaplan Newsweek: How to Get into College, 2001 Edition* (2000): 50–51.

The College Board. *Advanced Placement Program Bulletin for Students and Parents.* Princeton, N.J.: College Board, 1999.

———. "PSAT." At www.sat-acttestprep.com/psat.htm (accessed October 15, 2001).

Fiske, Edward B. *The Fiske Guide to Getting into the Right College.* New York: Times Books, 1997.

Hargadon, Fred. *A Letter to Prospective Applicants for the Class of '04.* Princeton, N.J.: Princeton University, 1999.

Harvard University. *Harvard for Entrance in Fall 2000.* Cambridge, Mass.: Harvard University, 2000.

———. *An Introduction to Harvard University.* Cambridge, Mass.: Harvard University, 1999.

Hernández, Michele A. *A Is for Admission: The Insider's Guide to Getting into the Ivy League and Other Top Colleges.* New York: Warner Books, 1997.

King, Patrick. "Big Crowd at a Tiny Door." *Kaplan Newsweek: How to Get into College, 2001 Edition* (2000): 37–38.

Krouse, Joe. "Letters of Credit: Choosing Your Backers." *Newsweek: How to Get into College, 1998 Edition* (1997): 56.

Meltzer, Tom. *Cracking the AP U.S. History.* New York: Princeton Review, 1999.

Nieuwenhuis, Marjorie. *A Parent's Guide to College Admissions: A Comprehensive Overview of What Parents Need to Know.* New York: Kaplan Books, 1997.

Official Visitors Guide to Boston and Its Top Colleges: Campus Visit. Boston: Hoffman, 1999.

The Peterson's Guide to Four-Year Colleges, 2000. 30th ed. Princeton, N.J.: Peterson's, 1999.

Princeton University. *Admission Information.* Princeton, N.J.: Princeton University, 1999–2000.

Sharpe, Rochelle. "Beating the Ivy League Odds." *Wall Street Journal,* April 16, 1999, W1.

Tse, May K. "An Insider's Look at MIT Admissions." *Tech* (Cambridge, Mass.), March 16, 1999, 6.

University of Virginia. *Prospectus.* Charlottesville: University of Virginia, 1999.

About the Authors

Bina Chandrasekhara has lived in Salisbury, Maryland, for over twenty years. She earned her master's degree in business administration at Salisbury University. She has worked at a bank in New York, but has dedicated most of her professional life to the daunting but rewarding tasks of raising children, volunteering at school, and serving the community. For over sixteen years Bina has been an active volunteer in school activities that include school improvement, fund-raising, and bus trips. For over eight years she has been particularly involved with her children's high school experience, dealing firsthand with the difficulties and challenges that led her to write this book. On the community front she has served as chairperson for the Maryland Food Bank as well as chairperson for the Kids Helping Kids program. She has also been a spokesperson representing the Eastern Shore of Maryland. She has served as a president and been an active member of the Wicomico County Medical Alliance board. Married for twenty-five years, she is the proud mother of two, Vinay and Sheila.

Vinay Chandrasekhara is currently a second-year medical student at the University of Virginia. He is the vice president of his class and a student representative of the basic science curriculum review committee. He graduated from the Massachusetts Institute of Technology with a major in biology and a minor in writing. While at MIT, he was a member of the freshman heavyweight crew team. Vinay was also the community service chair of several organizations, for which he organized campuswide service events for undergraduates to help the homeless and needy. He was an active volunteer for the Boston Marathon, yearly leading a team of undergraduates to work at water stations along the racecourse. During his spare time, Vinay also helped teach second-grade students in local public schools.

Sheila Chandrasekhara is a sophomore at Harvard University majoring in government. At school, Sheila is an active member of the Mock Trial team and is involved in City Step, a community service program that teaches children self-expression and self-confidence through dance. She is a recipient of the Girl Scouts Gold Award. She founded the Youth Foundation Fund in her hometown of Salisbury, Maryland, the mission of which is to help children by creating awareness of giving and by establishing and supporting organizations that promote youth betterment.

135